Mind-Play

Jerome L. Singer, Ph.D., is professor of psychology and director of the Clinical Psychology Training Program at Yale University. He received his doctorate at the University of Pennsylvania and was trained in psychoanalysis at the William Alanson White Institute in New York. A pioneer in research on imagination and daydreaming, he has published more than one hundred technical articles and several books in this field.

Ellen Switzer is a freelance writer specializing in psychology, law, and medicine. She is a contributing editor to *Family Circle* and a regular contributor to *Vogue, Self,* and *Working Woman.* She has been on the staff of *Time* and the *New York Herald Tribune,* and is author or coauthor of several books.

PRENTICE-HALL, INC., Englewood Cliffs, N.J. 07632

A SPECTRUM BOOK

JEROME L. SINGER
ELLEN SWITZER

Mind-Play

The Creative Uses of Fantasy

Library of Congress Cataloging in Publication Data

Singer, Jerome L.
    Mind-play.

    (A Spectrum Book)
    Bibliography: p.
    Includes index.
    1. Fantasy—Therapeutic use. 2. Success.
I. Switzer, Ellen Eichenwald, joint author.
II. Title.
RC489.F35S58   616.89'14   79-28296
ISBN 0-13-583369-8
ISBN 0-13-583351-5 pbk.

A SPECTRUM BOOK

Printed in the United States of America

10 9 8 7 6 5 4 3 2 1

Editorial/production supervision and interior design by Maria Carella.
Manufacturing buyer: Barbara A. Frick

Prentice-Hall International, Inc., *London*
Prentice-Hall of Australia Pty., Limited, *Sydney*
Prentice-Hall of Canada, Ltd., *Toronto*
Prentice-Hall of India Private, Limited, *New Delhi*
Prentice-Hall of Japan, Inc., *Tokyo*
Prentice-Hall of Southeast Asia Pte., Ltd., *Singapore*
Whitehall Books, Limited, *Wellington, New Zealand*

Contents

Mind-Play

1

Creative Daydreaming

Your imagination, your capacity to daydream or fantasize, to relive the past or probe the future through pictures in your mind's eye, is one of the greatest resources you have as a human being. Wired into the natural functioning of your brain there is a powerful resource for healthy escape, for self-entertainment, and for fuller and more effective living. Don't be afraid to daydream or to use your imagination because you fear that you'll lose touch with reality. You can learn to enjoy and to control the great powers of your imagination and from these inner resources you can often forge a better reality.

Let's take a look at some people from various walks of life and see how they are coping with or without the effective use of their imaginative powers.

Joan Anders is 24 years old, smart, and attractive, and she has an excellent job as assistant director on a TV news show. She is engaged to a young lawyer whom all her friends consider an outstanding candidate for her pretty hand. **2** Her feminist friends admire him because he seems as interested in her career as she is. Her traditional friends remark that he really seems to be a good catch (a remark that makes Joan furious, although she has never expressed her anger). Even her parents like him. It would seem that Joan is the original woman who has everything.

But Joan is actually anxious some of the time, bored much of the time, and thoroughly confused all of the time. She has trouble sleeping and a tendency to be overweight. When she's feeling insecure, she comforts herself with rich desserts, pasta al forno, and other calorie-laden foods. She is also an avid reader of popular psychological books and magazine articles and has diagnosed her problems at various times as free-floating anxiety, endogenous depression, phobia, and lack of assertive behavior. She has not sought professional help because her various troubles somehow don't seem serious enough to warrant psychotherapy, but she does take enough Valium in the course of a year to produce a sizable drugstore bill every month. When she is not taking Valium, she tries out various over-the-counter pills and capsules to help her sleep at night, perk her up in the morning, and help her stay on the diet that promised instant and permanent weight loss without hunger or discomfort.

Because of her devotion to self-help books, we firmly expect Joan to buy this book a week after it's published, but she won't recognize herself. Her case history, like all the others we shall be discussing, has been thoroughly disguised to protect her privacy.

Then there is Eleanor Beatty, 25, married to a high school English teacher, and the mother of three children under 8. Eleanor spends much of her time at repetitive and boring tasks. Her large, old, inconvenient house requires a great deal of effort to remain in reasonable order. Her husband and children seem to produce at least two loads of dirty laundry per day. The **3**

family is on a tight budget, so meal planning
and preparation is time-consuming. The children
need a good deal of transportation to Cub Scout
meetings, dentist appointments, and after-school
play at friends' houses; Eleanor spends at least
two hours every day chauffeuring her brood.

At first glance, Eleanor looks like a character
right out of a Betty Friedan or Gloria Steinem
nightmare. And there are times when she longs
for the life she had before she got married: teaching art at a junior college. Occasionally, as she
flicks through the pages of *Ms.* magazine, she
resents her house-bound, husband- and child-
centered existence and asks herself if there might
not be more to life than a round of unmade beds,
dirty dishes, meals to plan, and children to chauffeur. Then she realizes that, of course, there *is*
more to her life than the sum of all these repetitive chores. She loves her husband and the children,
and she knows that once her immediate child-
caring days are over, she can get back to the
teaching job she loved. Meanwhile, she is able to
entertain herself and to overcome her anxieties
and frustrations a great deal better than Joan
Anders, whose lifestyle she might well be expected
to envy.

John Powers, like Joan Anders, has a creative,
interesting job as an editor on a news magazine.
Like Eleanor, he has a home and three children.
But he is in worse shape then either of the two
women. He eats too much. He drinks too much.
His blood pressure is too high. His sex life with
his wife has become somewhat drab and routine,
and his affair with his secretary is causing him
more problems than pleasure. He seems to have a
certain amount of difficulty planning for the future, both in his work and in his personal life.
The consequences of his actions often surprise
him. He has discussed his problems with his physician, who has advised TM or some other kind of
structured relaxation exercises but does not feel
that John needs extensive psychotherapy to

restructure his life. "You seem to me to be bored and frustrated," he has told his patient. "Try to get yourself out of your present rut, and perhaps some of your symptoms will improve. If not, we can discuss therapy later."

You will be reading more about Joan, Eleanor, and John throughout this book, and you will also meet some other people who have problems: for instance, Andrea, who is thinking of converting to Hari Krishna, much to the horror of her Unitarian parents; Sylvia, who is terrified of flying and has just been promoted to a job which will inevitably include cross-country trips; David, who freezes at the very thought of an examination but who has decided to go to law school. Then there is Susan, who in spite of better than average intelligence and charm, cannot keep a job; and Maximilian, whose grandiose schemes usually end in disaster. Except for Eleanor, all of these people, and many more whom we will discuss, have one major characteristic in common: they are either incapable of daydreams and fantasy, or they are using these important life tools inappropriately or incorrectly.

The capacity for fantasy and daydreams may be our most human quality. It may also be evolution's greatest gift to us. Our fantasies and daydreams allow us to master our environment in ways that no other living being can. We can entertain ourselves, educate ourselves, change ourselves, comfort ourselves, and enrich our lives in an infinite variety of ways with nothing more than the material stored away in our own heads.

The human imagination, daydreams, night dreams, and fantasies represent a power for constructive living and self-fulfillment whose potential psychologists and scientists have only recently begun to grasp. We know that the capacity to produce vivid memories and images, to explore the past and the possible future, is a major psychological resource that most people do not use to full effect. Our ability to recall the past, reliving important moments in our lives, can enrich the present and also keep us from repeating destructive or mistaken patterns. We can research the future before it happens and thereby plan in a more constructive, creative way. We can even play with impossibilities, dream of being someone we can never be in real life, accomplish feats of intellect and daring we obviously will never achieve, and build a bright and happy world even when all around us life seems bleak and uninteresting.

Somehow, daydreaming has managed to get a bad name. Parents warn their children not to waste time wool-gathering. Horatio Alger's heroes, after all, did not spend their time fantasizing. They got right out there and rescued the boss's daughter from a runaway horse, put in countless hours of extra work, and in their spare time polished the knocker on the old brass door to assure for themselves the kind of material success they were seeking. Hard work and no illusions are basic to the Puritan ethic by which most of us have been taught to live.

Even psychiatrists and psychologists who can see flaws in the Puritan ethic sometimes consider daydreams a waste of time and psychic energy, or even a symptom of mental or emotional problems. Sigmund Freud, for instance, said: "Happy people do not make fantasies...only unsatisfied ones do." And yet he used fantasies and dreams (day and night) as an integral part of his therapy technique.

Some researchers in the past may have ignored the importance of fantasy to mental health because they thought of it in terms of hallucinations (hearing voices and seeing objects that are not there) or delusions (believing that one is Napoleon or Marilyn Monroe). These, of course, *are* symptoms of mental illness. Someone who is firmly convinced that forces from outer space or the CIA are controlling him with buzzing wires in the wall actually hears those wires buzz. No

amount of rational argument will change such a

person's mind. Someone who is convinced that she is a famous movie star or the Queen of Holland won't be convinced that this is not so by being confronted with her own image in the mirror or by being reminded that she does not speak a word of Dutch. Someone who believes that he is Robert Redford or Henry Kissinger won't change his mind because obvious facts contradict the illusion. In literature we sometimes find characters whose inner reality has become blurred in this way. Blanche DuBois in Tennessee Williams's *A Streetcar Named Desire* is a perfect example of such confusion: she escaped the unhappiness of a middle-aged life filled with dying relatives by convincing herself she was a fine, young Southern lady with dozens of suitors. When brutally confronted with the true circumstances of her existence by her insensitive brother-in-law, she retreated entirely into her delusions.

But there is no real danger that this could happen to a mentally healthy person with an active fantasy life. The daydreamer, unlike the mentally ill patient, knows the boundaries between fantasy and reality. The evidence indicates that fantasy can actually be helpful in allowing us to test the boundaries between what is real and what is imagined. We can teach ourselves to turn our fantasies on and off, like a videotape machine. We can travel easily between the world of dreams and the world of reality, without confusing one with the other. And there is no contradiction between what we consider rational thought and what we think of as fantasy. The most productive kind of thinking will probably have an element of fantasy in it. We don't literally respond to all the cues in our environment. We sort them through and ascribe various values and consequences to them. This often means playing out in our minds a variety of possible alternatives, that is, engaging in daydreaming. People who lack this ability, who give equal importance to all cues, would tend to live in a "Mary Hartman, Mary Hartman" kind of world. Poor

7

Mary is totally confused by life because she has
no imagination at all. She believes everything she
hears and reads with a total lack of discrimination,
so the yellow wax buildup on her kitchen floor
and the activities of a mass murderer in the neighborhood seem equally threatening. As a television
character her literal, unimaginative interpretation
of everything around her makes her a very comic
figure. In real life, she'd be a tragic one.

Mental health professionals also have tended
to ascribe a higher value to verbal language processes than to auditory or visual imagery. This prejudice is so pervasive probably because most of us
depend on verbal expression for communication.
But why should the brain of a Beethoven or Bach—
teeming with melody, with novel and original
combinations and themes, instrumental colorations
and interweaving lines of music— be viewed as representing a more primitive style of thought than
the mind of a mathematician mentally solving alge-
bra problems.

Important recent discoveries in brain research,
as well as studies of information processing, have
shown us that two separate hemispheres of the
brain function in separate but equally important
and cooperative ways. The left hemisphere deals
with what we tend to call "rational" material,
receptive and expressive language, mathematics,
and the like. The function of the right side includes
visual and auditory imagery, spatial representation,
pure melodic thought, fantasy, and what scientists
call "emotional components of ongoing thought,"
that is, the ability to look ahead and backwards
in images and sounds rather than in words. We
know something about the stream of consciousness
through writers like Virginia Woolf and James
Joyce. Obviously, the content of this stream *must*
be conveyed in words, since that is the only way
it can be communicated to the reader. But the
8 really gifted writer is able to evoke, through words,

the kinds of images that run through the characters' minds as they reveal their inner lives.

Actually, even those of us who do not have the gift of poetic fancy use words in this way in our daily lives. For instance, one might take the following abstract assertion: "The consequences of our actions evoked the wrath of the authorities." If, instead, we substitute the metaphor: "That's when the shit hit the fan," and try further to imagine it vividly through each sense—sight, sound, smell, touch, and taste,—the consequences of shit hitting a fan can certainly invoke the *emotional* experience of bringing down on oneself the wrath of the authorities.

The natural function of the human brain itself creates great possibilities within us. Our brain stores literally millions of scenes, events, conversations, and stories which we have lived through, read about, heard, or witnessed second-hand through the movies or television. The brain replays this material, over and over, in constantly new variations. The fascinating variety of our dreams night after night can give us a limited idea of the vast movie or television industry that lies within us and that we can learn to control. Nor do we need to take drugs or involve ourselves in the elaborate rituals of exotic religious sects to harness our daydream power. Psychological research has pointed to dozens of practical steps each of us can take to gain more effective control of our imaginative potential. Instead of dismissing our daydreams as childish and frivolous, we can learn to make them work for us in real life. Our daydreams are not simply an escape from the trials and tribulations of the workaday world, although they can be used for such an escape to good effect. They also point toward practical approaches of solving our problems. They free us from the stranglehold of schedules and the inevitable passage of time. We can move back through **9**

the past and far into the future within seconds
without risking any commitments. Daydreams
represent a form of trial action by which we can
circumvent space and time, and explore the possibilities of life.

John Powers, who finds it so difficult to plan
for the future and who makes mistakes because he
cannot picture the consequences of his actions,
would probably be able to improve his life if he
allowed his fantasy a freer flow. He would be able
to rehearse in his mind the various options that
present themselves, and this in itself would make
planning much easier for him. He would also be
able to picture in his mind how others might react
to his sometimes thoughtless activities and so mini-
mize and even eliminate some mistakes.

Daydreams and night dreams probably can't
predict the future as many of our ancestors believed, and as some of us still do, but they can
point the way for us to change our future in a
constructive and realistic fashion.

Do all of us daydream at times? With a few
exceptions, probably yes. After all, our daydreams
are, in a sense, extensions of our childhood capacity for play. A child who is unable to pretend,
unable to use his or her imagination, is rare, and
probably sick. We can continue in the spirit of
childhood play and use it for many purposes in
daily life. Of course, we have to build into our
fantasies a self-checking system that will keep us
from becoming so involved with our inner world
that we miss important clues from the outer one.
We don't want to let our fantasy wander through
calm and beautiful mountain trails while we are
driving a car along a superhighway. Successful
daydreaming lies in a smooth shifting from external awareness to inner concentration.

Eleanor Beatty is able to do this and that is
the reason she is able to perform routine tasks
with a minimum of boredom. If her present becomes too oppressive, she can allow her mind to
range over interesting scenes of the past and hope-

ful scenes of the future. In this way, she can eliminate anxiety and boredom, as well as make realistic plans for the kind of life she will lead when her children are older.

If we have been conditioned to distrust our fantasies and to eliminate them from our lives, we are missing a great deal of potential joy. It's necessary even for the person who feels guilty about every "wasted" minute to allow him or herself the luxury of a trip through an imaginary world. In order to do this, of course, it's important to stop feeling guilty about letting one's mind wander occasionally.

Joan Anders is the kind of person who considers all daydreams a waste of time. She feels constantly under tension because she rushes through her days concentrating only on the next hour's immediate problem. Because she finds it so difficult to let her imagination roam over her own future, that is, married life with her fiancé, the idea of any change tends to terrify her. It is as if she were expected to take a trip into a strange country without knowing that country's language or customs.

There are many other ways in which fantasy and daydreams could help Joan, Eleanor and John, and we'll discuss them later in this book. We hope this book will persuade even the most achievement-oriented executive or hard-working, hard-driving professional or dedicated, busy homemaker that *fantasy and daydreams will not only enrich his or her life, but will also lead to more creative thought, more fun, and better physical and emotional health.*

Here are just a few of the benefits that daydreams can bring into your life:

Our imagery can help us to reduce stress.
We all know that stress is bad for our health. It can cause such minor physical ills as headaches and such serious diseases as hypertension and cardiac problems. Some so-called primitive societies have long used fantasies and daydreams to

11

reduce stress. In recent years, scientists have re-discovered some of these methods to help us overcome the pressures of our everyday life. For instance, patients with migraines, high blood pressure, or ulcers have been urged by their physicians to use meditation techniques for relaxation. Some of the most effective of these techniques use an organized system of daydreaming or fantasy.

Daydreams can often help us plan a more effective future.

In our minds, we can rehearse actions we may wish to take in the future, as well as review actions we may have taken in the past. In that way, we are often able to decide what has been or will be constructive and creative, and what has been or will be destructive or self-defeating.

Our imagery can help us gain control over undesirable habits.

Various psychological techniques, used with great effectiveness by a variety of therapists, encourage us to combine relaxation with controlled fantasy to help us give up habits and impulses which are harmful. It is possible to learn some of these techniques on our own for dealing with such problems as excessive smoking, over-eating, or nail-biting.

Our fantasies can help us to become more sensitive to the moods and needs of others.

We are often told that we cannot understand others unless we have "walked a mile in their moccasins." Obviously, this kind of empathy requires a trained and active imagination. In our fantasies we can put ourselves into another person's footwear and find out whether the emotional shoe feels comfortable or pinches.

Our daydreams can help us to increase our sexual pleasure.

12   The new sex therapies use many kinds of

mind trips to help inhibited or frightened people overcome hangups. Even for someone whose sex life is already fulfilling and satisfying, the addition of erotic fantasy provides occasional variety and excitement.

Our imagination can enhance our creativity in daily living as well as in artistic and scientific expression.

Most of us would agree that fantasy is an indispensable ingredient in any kind of artistic endeavor. However, it is equally valuable in the kind of thinking that produces important scientific advances. Stretching an idea to one's outer limits can open up new and unsuspected vistas.

Our fantasies and daydreams can help us to learn more about ourselves.

We all carry convictions about the kind of person we *ought* to be. Often these convictions can obscure, in our own minds, the kind of person we really are. We can use our fantasies and daydreams to spot hidden areas of ourselves, to illuminate parts that we may not have known existed. And as we get to know ourselves better, we can adopt more appropriate methods of living.

Our daydreams can help us to amuse ourselves in idle moments.

All of us spend time waiting. It's part of the world we live in. That's why doctors, lawyers, accountants, beauty parlors, and even the IRS keep magazines in their outer offices. But often the literature we find there is uninteresting, and the receptionist is too busy to exchange pleasantries about the weather. So coming fully equipped with a number of appropriate fantasies will help us to while away the time. Not only that, they will help us to overcome impatience and even fear of what's going to happen to us once the wait is over. **13**

Fantasizing can help us avoid boredom.
There are people who will tell us (whether we want to know or not) that they are absolutely, positively *never* bored. Lack of boredom becomes an emotional status symbol. But there are very few of us who don't occasionally experience some twinges of boredom, and we can put daydreams and fantasies to work to overcome them.

Our images and daydreams can help heighten our enjoyment of art, literature, music, theatre, and films.
Almost all forms of artistic expression require us to add our own imagination to that of the artist. Of course, when we read we have to translate the verbal impressions into sensual ones in order to give additional dimension to the written word. But we can also add our own personal touches to the paintings or films we see and the music to which we listen. Our imagination can even heighten the pleasure of a good meal by bringing back the memory of fine food we have enjoyed in the past.

Daydreaming and reminiscing can help us to deal effectively with the loneliness of old age and can even make it possible to confront our own death with dignity.
Everything we have learned in life, all the impressions we have stored in our brain, can be recalled over and over again. The past can be a great comfort when the present looks bleak and the future seems empty.

Our lives can be vastly enriched if we attend to our private processes and allow ourselves the leisure of playing them out for a few minutes every day. Once we realize the importance of fantasy and daydreams, we may decide to actually plan time for such activities in our daily lives. To do this, we have to sit quietly for a few minutes each day, probably looking into space with our eyes shut or focusing on a blank wall, deliber-

14

ately allowing our memories, wishes, and impressions to surface in our minds. We might want to do this on awakening in the morning, possibly reviewing our dreams from the night before. Or we might take time out during a busy day to recollect or anticipate exciting experiences and events. Usually this experience relaxes and refreshes us and allows us to attack our immediate problems with new vigor.

Nor will all our fantasies be pleasant ones. Attention to our experiences and dreams brings us into contact with our past doubts and failures, with the pettiness and evil within all of us. Every day we certainly face the possibility of danger as well as with pleasure. We can call up many horrors, including the inevitability of the death of someone we love or of our own death. In a way, this activity prepares us for what will happen in the future.

The daydreamer is not unaware of suffering and of the tragedy inherent in life itself. But greater enrichment is also part of our human potential, and daydreaming is the fundamental means of such enrichment. The practiced daydreamer has, in a way, the best and the worst of two opposite worlds. The increased inner capacity offers us a fuller sense of being alive from moment to moment, even though pain as well as pleasure is a part of that self-awareness.

Fantasy:
A Foundation
for Serenity

There is a Hari Krishna Temple down the street and 16-year-old Andrea wants to join. Her parents are appalled. They claim she's been brainwashed. Fifteen-year-old Greg is considering joining Reverend Moon's crusade. His parents are trying to make up their minds whether to send him to a psychiatrist or to a boarding school. However, Andrea's mother swears that two weekends of EST have changed her life, and Greg's father has been taking six Valium a day in order to keep on an even keel.

Americans, perhaps more than any other group tend to look for peace of mind outside of themselves. Many of us seem to believe that someone, somewhere knows the secret of happiness and that if we can just find the right source, results will be guaranteed. So the tranquilizers, Valium and Librium are the most frequently prescribed drugs in the United States. And every two years or so a new guru becomes fashionable. Dress designers and motion picture stars visit him at his ashram in India. Thousands of others listen to his disciples in crowded hotel dining rooms.

Meanwhile, children have their own gurus and their own drugs. The drugs tend to be illegal ones, such as marijuana and cocaine, and the gurus tend to be more bizarre than those of their parents. The motivation is basically the same, but the difference serves to widen the generation gap.

Yet, personal experience and research have shown that we all have a neglected resource inside our heads that might eliminate the need for outside stimulation through drugs or magic rituals. Fantasy and daydreams, far from being irrelevant and insubstantial, may be the foundation of serenity and purpose in our lives. Many recent experiments with people who use drugs and alcohol to stimulate or numb their inner lives suggest that fantasy can play an important role in the healthy development of any man or woman. Those who have trouble using fantasy to enrich their experiences or as a substitute for aggression run the risk of serious trouble at each stage of their lives.

You may have observed that unimaginative people become easily bored. They also tend to be less relaxed than highly imaginative people. What the various kinds of "psychological" group experiences such as EST or certain kinds of encounter groups often provide is a substitute for fantasy. All these methods lean on the ability of the charismatic leader to produce certain mind images which may provide temporary escape from boredom and loneliness. The gurus our children follow tend to work in a similar way. It's possible that the youngsters are not "brainwashed" at all; they may just use the prefabricated message of the cult leader to fill in empty spaces in their minds left by the lack of an active fantasy life.

Only the most fanatic behavioral scientist would argue that our reactions and attitudes are determined solely by the environment. The cognitive movement in psychology has reaffirmed the ancient image of human beings as thoughtful, curious, purposeful creatures. We bring to each 19 new situation certain expectations that influence our response to a given environment: our fantasies, our memories, our private commentary on what is happening with other people and with the inanimate world. If, however, we suppress our daydreams and fantasies, we may find that the world has gone flat, that we do not have the interest or zest to make the most of what our environment has to offer. It is then that we seek to bring in color and flavor through drugs, alcohol, or rituals.

Jerome L. Singer and Judith Rodin at Yale University and Stanley Schachter at Columbia University, among others, have conducted recent experiments with drug addicts and chronic overeaters. These experiments have revealed that some of these addicted individuals seem to respond only to external stimulation. For them, the social and physical environment seems to say: "Eat me! Drink me! Touch me! Kiss me!"—and they simply cannot resist such appeals. Such an excessive sensitivity to external stimulation can, of course, lead to troubles, such as obesity, alcoholism, and even jail terms for disturbing the peace.

An effective method of separating imaginative persons from relatively unimaginative ones was developed by a psychiatrist, Hermann Rorschach, just after World War I. His inkblot pictures are still used today. Rorschach found that some people, when asked what they saw in the ambiguous inkspots, were much more likely than others to associate them with human figures in action, instead of inanimate objects. These people tended to be more imaginative. They were also more controlled than persons who did not see moving human figures.

In effect, Rorschach was proposing that if you present a person with an inkblot, and he or she responds by describing a scene of lively human activity, that individual probably tends generally to heed the movements and imaginings of his or her inner eye. By contrast, those who don't take

20 the trouble to organize the inkblots into personal

images and who respond only to obvious charac- teristics, such as color or the black blots' resemblance to bats, are more likely to be impulsive and excessively dependent on the external environment.

One of the reasons the Rorschach tests are still used so extensively is that a large body of research supports Rorschach's view. The great developmental psychologist, Heinz Werner, for instance, discovered years ago that hyperactive retarded children were not as likely to see movement in the inkblots as more relaxed ones. The same distinction applies to normal children. Dr. Anneliese Riess at New York University watched kindergarten children who were left alone in the waiting room. The children who showed little imagination in their inkblot readings were the ones who also could not sit still.

Even children as young as 3 or 4 are likely to be more restless if their Rorschach responses are unimaginative. This tendency becomes more pronounced in older children and preadolescents: those who lack imagination, also tend to be more aggressive. Also, they are more likely than their imaginative peers to imitate a teacher directly, rather than to use their own experiences, fantasies, and memories at school. They may do well in spelling and learning arithmetic tables. They may even have exceedingly neat handwriting. But they lack the originality that may make the difference between a plodder and an inspired student. The same, incidentally, is probably also true of their teachers.

Children of equal intelligence but unequal imaginations also differ in their sensitivity to reality. We often assume that children with an active fantasy life have a weaker grasp on hard facts than their more pedestrian brothers and sisters. Exactly the opposite is true. Research shows that children whose games are lacking in make-believe and fantasy are likely to have trouble recalling and integrating the details of events they hear about. So the imaginative youngsters **21** may do better at many school tasks that go beyond rote memory than their less imaginative classmate.

From childhood on, imagination seems to be a vital human capacity. A well-developed fantasy life seems to be partly responsible for independence, tranquility, and realism.

The restlessness and dependence on the physical environment that we see in more unimaginative children can become a more serious problem in adolescence. Imaginative young people seem to internalize the faces and voices of adults which warn, "Be careful!" and which ask, "Is this really what you want?" But adolescents who are troublemakers or delinquents seem not to hear these inner voices. Their early contacts with adults just did not teach them to play out in their fantasy the complex and relatively self-controlled behavior of their elders.

This theory too is borne out by research. In 1949 William Goldfarb compared children who had been brought up in old-fashioned orphanages to those who had been reared in families. The children who grew up in institutions had much less imagination. They also tended to have much more extreme reactions, often aggressive ones, whenever their social or physical environment was changed. The ability to adapt to change without becoming emotionally disturbed is obviously one of the most useful qualities children will need in their adult lives.

Much more recently, psychologist Leonard Goldberg, at the City College of New York, found that imaginative children at a child guidance clinic were less likely to be violent than other children. They were as emotionally troubled as the rest of the youngsters in the clinic, but they showed this in less aggressive ways than their unimaginative peers.

George Spivack and Murray Levine, working in a school for emotionally troubled children in Pennsylvania, discovered comparable tendencies among middle-class adolescents. When asked to complete a story, delinquent youths tended to rush the narrative through to the end without considering the conflicts or precautions that their version of the story would almost invariably entail. They also seemed less aware than nondelinquents when they broke the rules of society. The nondelinquents who also thought and talked about breaking the rules were nonetheless more aware of the pros and cons of their proposals. They kept a sharp eye out for loopholes in the rules, however, so that they might possibly get their own way without running into trouble.

On the Rorschach inkblot test, the delinquent group seemed consistently less imaginative than the others. Spivack wrote: "Their thought world appears a rather barren place."

The same unimaginative group of middle-class youngsters, when asked about their families, appeared to be uninformed about, as well as insensitive to, their family backgrounds and histories. They were even a little fuzzy about what their fathers did for a living. They seemed to have interacted so little with their parents that they had not been able to adopt adult attitudes. Instead, they took their cues from other children, usually the ones immediately around them.

Research with adults reveals a similar correlation between imagination and the control of impulsive and/or aggressive behavior.

Normal adults who can see little human movement in the inkblots also tend to react quickly and impulsively to ambiguous environmental clues, whether in the test itself or in other situations. On tests of free association, for instance, unimaginative adults react to the cue words by saying the first thing that pops into their heads. Such people often mention physical objects in the room, for instance, rather than any association from their own memories. Their inner experiences seem less important to them than even the most irrelevant fact of their immediate environment.

Even the behavior of schizophrenics seems to 23

vary according to how imaginative their Rorschach responses are. In one experiment, relatively unimaginative schizophrenic patients, left alone in a waiting room for 15 minutes, paced restlessly up and down and picked up various games and puzzles at random, putting them down again without using them. Imaginative patients sat quietly, apparently in thought, or worked at a puzzle until they had solved it.

A study of criminals in Florida also points to a link between lack of imagination and aggression. A group of habitually violent criminals proved in tests to be less imaginative than criminals who were much less violent.

But most of us are neither psychological test subjects, nor schizophrenics, nor criminals, violent or otherwise. So how does all of this apply to us? Principally in that all of us have to control our aggressions and our impulses if we wish to lead reasonably happy and productive lives. Persons who blow up at their bosses consistently because they have not learned to control aggressive impulses usually spend a good deal of time unemployed. The husband, wife, father, or mother who can deal with a conflict only by turning it into a shouting match may end up with a marriage counselor or in a divorce court. Obviously it is preferable to work out these conflicts in one's mind rather than in real life where others can be hurt or impulsive actions cannot be taken back.

Failure to use one's imagination may lead to other problems besides boredom and aggression. In Chapter 7 we shall be discussing the concept of fantasy as an adjunct to successful dieting for weight loss. But two studies dealing with overeating seem relevant here. Psychologist Stanley Schachter and his co-workers at Columbia have demonstrated that people who eat too much seem to have trouble resisting food when it's placed in front of them. They tend to ignore other cues from their external environment, such as the

24 Weight Watcher's diet in the kitchen drawer.

In one experiment with both overweight and normal men during a religious fast when no food was in sight, the comparatively slender men suffered much more from hunger than the fat men. It seems that fat men without the external stimulation of seeing food do not feel hungry.

In a related study of overweight male college students carried out by Jerome L. Singer and Judith Rodin at Yale University, the researchers tried to discover whether the subjects' general tendency to overeat might reflect some failure of the imagination. It was discovered that, although fat students liked to daydream as much as their slender peers, they experienced significantly less visual imagery in their fantasies. What's more, when they tried to summon memories or generate fantasies with another person, the overweight students tended to shut their eyes. Apparently they had to blank out the external environment because it was too distracting. This relative weakness of their imaginations might account for the excessive responsiveness when actual food—a cue from the external environment—was placed in front of them.

A similar process may be involved in the use of certain drugs. Recently one of the co-authors was involved in a study with George Huba and Bernard Segal that compared drug and alcohol use with daydreaming and personality. More than a thousand college students and military recruits took part. They were divided into four groups: those who used alcohol only, those who used marijuana only, those who used neither alcohol nor marijuana, and those who used several different drugs, particularly hard drugs such as heroin, cocaine, and LSD.

The young drug and alcohol users, it was found, were likely to be "externalizers," that is they sought outside stimulation. They were more interested in trying out different lifestyles than in elaborating on different fantasies, and they also tended to be restless and impulsive (confirming

25

the earlier studies on children, convicts, and
schizophrenics). In addition, it was learned that
drug and alcohol users tend to be more subject to
boredom and mind wandering than nonusers, and
their fantasies, though frequent, tend to be fleeting
and undeveloped. By contrast, people who abstain
from alcohol and drugs appear to be more orderly,
more interested in achievement, and more concerned with the future. Their daydreams reflect
these tendencies.

Psychological tests have revealed consistent
differences among drug users and nonusers. The
differences were true for both sexes in each of several colleges that were visited by Drs. Segal, Huba,
and Singer.

In other research studies by the three doctors
named above, it was noted that the users of hard
drugs fall into two groups. One seemed to want to
escape from external pressures or distressing,
poorly controlled inner fantasies. They sought
numbness and chose barbiturates and other de-
pressants to achieve it. The second group were
more interested in finding new external stimulation. Their favorite drugs were amphetamines and
similar stimulants. But these hard drug users were
less likely than soft drug users to have rich daydreams or to use their fantasies to solve problems.
They preferred a mildly disorganized, pleasure-
oriented, hang-loose existence.

Drug users, in spite of what they may tell us,
don't seem to be particularly interested in inner
consciousness. This fact should dispel any lingering
romantic notion that drugs attract individuals
with a yearning for deep insight. On the contrary,
the drinkers and users of hard drugs can be described as people who have failed to develop an
elaborate, satisfying inner fantasy life. They are
restless and impulsive, searching endlessly for new
experiences, even when their search may be harmful to their physical and mental health. They seem
to want autonomy but have little sense of the
26 planning and slow achievement that might win

them real personal freedom. Lacking the ability to try out, in their minds, a range of possibilities, they seem to be victims of external forces—whether drugs, sights and sounds, other people, or strange and ritualistic cults. They lack the inner control and quiet sense of purpose that a rich imagination can provide.

Obviously, we cannot guarantee that learning to use one's daydreams or fantasies will necessarily or automatically provide serenity. It won't. But research indicates that a vivid imagination can, indeed, help us to a richer, calmer, and more serene life.

How to Improve Your Daydreaming Capacity

Some people will read the preceding chapter and say, "All this is fine and good, but I for one don't daydream at all." Usually they will add, with a certain amount of pride, that they don't dream at night either. What such people are really saying is that they are objective, businesslike individuals who may be trusted not to take off for fantasy land when there's work to be done.

Let's start out by demolishing the myth that some people never dream at all. Probably even the sternest, most prosaic individual can be placed in a sleep laboratory and attached to an electro-encephalograph (a brain wave machine, EEG for short) and have the instrument show dream activity. He or she may assure everybody on awakening that the sleep was completely dreamless, but proof that it was not shows literally in black and white on the brain wave tracing. Practically everybody when awakened during so-called Rapid Eye Movement sleep in the laboratory does report that he or she was dreaming or thinking. Almost everybody dreams even though some people just forget their dreams the second after they have awakened.

30

It's also just about impossible to go through life without daydreaming. Any review of the past, any planning for the future, involves daydreams. The persons who insist that they never daydream may actually be saying that they don't indulge in what they would consider idle fantasy. Or else they've practiced *ignoring* these experiences and often shift their attention to outside situations when they do catch themselves in a "brown study."

Those who are proud of their ability to fantasize might sit in a comfortable chair calling up images of mountain meadows in Switzerland or waterfalls in Jamaica. Bottom-line people might sit in straight-backed chairs at their desks and picture steeply rising sales graphs in their minds. Both kinds of persons are, of course, daydreaming.

We hope that we have by now established that just about all of us are capable of using our imagination to improve the quality of our lives. But there are people who find it more difficult than others to let their imaginations lead them. They are usually individuals who have always prided themselves on their precise, organized way of thinking and have not allowed themselves the luxury of dipping into the natural flow of ongoing consciousness. These people can be taught to sharpen their daydreaming ability. Even people who have a great deal of imagination could probably benefit from further practice. Here are some simple exercises that should improve your ability to daydream and show you how to use your imagination constructively:

1. Keep a record of night dreams and daydreams. Journal keeping has become a popular activity. Some especially imaginative journal keepers turn their records into fiction; some, like Erica Jong, write million-dollar best sellers. Others just keep them locked away and use them as a sort of paper psychiatrist, to calm themselves down, rev **31**

themselves up, or just entertain themselves. Many of us as preadolescents kept "diaries" that contained as much fantasy as real experiences, although we didn't label them daydreams. We tried to tell ourselves that the football captain, or the gorgeous young French teacher, were *really* secretly in love with us, although, of course, deep down inside we knew better.

As adults, we can keep journals of our fantasies and daydreams, clearly labeled as such in our conscious and unconscious minds.

2. After writing down a daydream or night dream, replay it in your mind as vividly as possible. Imagine that the inside of your head is a videotape machine. You can rewind it and start all over again any time you want to. Try to do this several times with the same dream. Of course, it helps to pick a pleasant one. An unpleasant dream could put you in a rotten mood for the rest of the day.

3. Look at a painting or a photograph, and then look away, preferably at a blank wall. Try to reproduce that picture as accurately as possible. Call up the shapes and colors. Trace them on the blank wall with your eyes. Use a simple picture first. Brightly colored abstract shapes like those in a Calder or a Miro lithograph work very well. Don't get discouraged if the image you produce in your mind's eye is relatively vague when you compare it to the real picture. Mental imagery is almost always somewhat fuzzy and unclear when compared with the real thing.

It may help if you shut your eyes while you are attempting to project the picture, but only if it feels comfortable to you. Concentrating and straining to keep your eyes squeezed shut tightly will only be self-defeating. You may want to try one of those sleep masks that Henry Kissinger used to wear on shuttle diplomacy trips to the Middle East. They are available in most drug and department stores. The reason for covering or

32

closing your eyes is that the real images you see, including even that blank wall, are distractions. The way to get the best kind of mind imagery is to be relaxed but still in control of what you want to project, and to have as few outside stimuli as possible interfering with your concentration.

Eventually, this may work so well that you will hardly be able to tell the difference between the real picture and the imagined one. A psychologist, the late Dr. Sydney Segal, did a series of experiments in which she had people imagine various simple objects: a ripe red tomato or a red and green apple, for instance. Her research subjects faced a blank screen. As the individuals imagined these objects, she would project slides of tomatoes or apples on the screen at the same point on which the subjects had been asked to fix their eyes. Surprisingly enough, many of these people could not tell when a real picture was flashed on the screen. They were so caught up in their own imagery that they were prevented from seeing the flash card.

Dr. Segal conducted these experiments in connection with research for the United States Air Force. There had been several incidents in which pilots thought they saw landing strips or a certain array of lights that were not really there. Her conclusion was that a person who is looking for something intently enough may actually believe that he or she is seeing it. This is why some of those pilots would try to land their planes before the landing strip was really visible. Expecting to see a pattern of lights, they might project so vivid a private image that they could blot out awareness of the "real" stimulus from the airport.

The same psychological phenomenon may explain why some earnest, truthful individuals are absolutely convinced that they have *seen* flying saucers; or why others see mirages of green and shady oases while they are in the middle of a desert sandstorm. We don't want to encourage people to see mirages, or for that matter landing

33

strips, but tomatoes on a blank screen would seem to be quite harmless and fun. If bananas are your thing, try those.

4. After you've sharpened your skills with still pictures, try moving ones. Recall a scene from the past that you especially enjoyed. Or replay a part of a motion picture or TV show that you liked. Project those scenes, movement and all, on the blank wall. If you are by yourself or with someone to whom you can confide what you are trying to do, you may want to attempt moving around as if you were actually *in* the scene. Of course, if you do this in a room full of strangers, they will probably think that you are more than a little peculiar. But moving along with the mind imagery sometimes helps to make it more vivid.

Again, your mind movies will probably not be as vivid or move in as consistent a manner as the real thing. But with practice, you'll probably be able to improve them a great deal.

5. Try to discover what kinds of scenes you can imagine most easily. Both the co-authors find that images with people in them arise most frequently. But an engineer or an architect might see complicated geometric forms which they can manipulate mentally. Start with what comes easiest to you and gradually work up to some of the harder scenes.

6. As you start to project images, try to sharpen them as much as possible. Dream up a person from your past, your third grade teacher, for instance. Fill in the fuzzy outlines. Was she fat or thin? What color was her hair? What dress do you remember her wearing most often? Did she wave her hands when she spoke? Did she pace up and down? After a while, you will probably be able to project a rather complete, detailed image of that teacher. The next time you try, you may be able to come up with a much more detailed picture in your mind without having to ask yourself all these questions first.

7. Picture a scene in which you may become involved in the future. Try something simple first. Let's say that you have an appointment with a vacuum cleaner salesman next week. Imagine yourself sitting on a chair reading the newspaper as the doorbell rings and the salesman walks in. Try to picture him in detail. (It does not matter if he turns out to look entirely different from what you have imagined. You are not trying to predict the future.) Then conduct an imaginary conversation with him. Go through the whole scenario as if you were actually writing a movie script. You can set up all the possibilities. He tries to get you to buy a certain vacuum cleaner that you don't want. You listen to his high-pressure sales talk and decide you don't want to buy. Or he quotes too high a price and you convince him to give you a discount. Of course, you have more control over scenes you are writing and directing in your mind than over real-life ones. But you can use this daydream experience to train yourself to be more effective when the future event actually happens. People with absolutely no sales resistance have used this kind of technique to learn how to turn down overeager salespeople, for instance.

8. Daydreams and fantasies do occasionally seem to have some life of their own, so the situation you imagined may not work out quite as you might have expected or wished. In that case, make some changes in the situation. That's one of the advantages fantasy has over real life. You can always adjust the people or objects to meet your particular needs. For instance, if you find that even in your fantasy you can't resist that salesman, picture him as looking like Groucho Marx or Peter Sellers. You almost certainly can resist a comic sales pitch, can't you? Or you might imagine that the whole situation is utterly wild, like a scene out of *Alice in Wonderland,* in which you point a **35**

finger and the salesman disappears in a puff of smoke.

9. Imagine a situation that you would like to have happen but that is fairly unlikely in real life. For instance, you have been invited to a pork barbecue at Jimmy Carter's home in Plains, Georgia, or to tea with Queen Elizabeth at Buckingham Palace. Or picture yourself walking down a street in New York and meeting Robert Redford or Raquel Welch; they are so impressed with your charm and intelligence that they strike up conversation and suggest going out to dinner. Try to work out an internal movie script, complete with details.

10. Read some fiction that is reasonably well written. Try to get yourself more deeply into the quality of the writing. Start with a short story and try to imagine yourself, as vividly as possible, in the situation of the characters. Imagine yourself in that setting, picturing it in your mind as if you were running through a television representation of what the writer has put down. You will often be able to translate the writer's imagery into your own by looking carefully at the choice of words the author has used. Get completely absorbed and then step back from the situation and then create your own mental pictures as vividly as you can.

Some readers like to imagine new endings for stories they have liked. Or they try to project an ending of their own before they have finished the book. That is, of course, the whole basis on which mystery stories are written. But one writer, John Fowles, in his novel *The French Lieutenant's Woman*, actually wrote several endings and invited the reader to pick out the one that seemed best. "If you had been the hero (or heroine) what would you have done?" he asked. "What seems most logical to you?"

11. Take a situation which may happen in the future and which might turn out to be somewhat unpleasant. You have to tell your employer that

you need a leave of absence, or you have to go visit Great Aunt Minnie who always makes you feel uncomfortable. Fantasy and imagery can help you to make these situations less threatening and worrisome. Humor will work as well here as it did in the vacuum salesman scenario. In the middle of berating you for wanting to leave in the middle of the busy season, your boss notices that he's still wearing his pajamas, for instance. Or your Aunt Minnie, after having asked you for the tenth time this year why a nice guy (or girl) like you is not married, suddenly confides that she has hidden $100,000 worth of gold coins under the mattress which she plans to drop down on your house by parachute as soon as you get married.

Of course, there are genuinely sad occasions in which this kind of imagery will seem inappropriate. But in most instances you can use fantasy and imagery to prepare yourself, to calm yourself, and to stop yourself from worrying unnecessarily.

The best humorists take a situation that is not only commonplace, but often potentially tragic, and give it a little twist that makes it funny. What goes on in your mind can't hurt anyone because it is not real. The same, of course, is true for comedy. If you worried about all those people in the movies or on television who get banana cream pies thrown in their faces or who slip on banana peels, you would find it impossible to laugh. But you know it's only make-believe, so it's funny. The same is true for your own fantasy scenes.

Once you have trained yourself to project vivid mind scenes, you will be able to entertain yourself, to remove yourself from irritating or boring situations, and to distract yourself from unnecessarily painful ones. Actually, that is the principle on which the technique of hypnosis is based.

Many people believe that hypnosis is a sort of mystical state, a mysterious condition that requires all kinds of special gadgets to be successful. **37**

Many people imagine a hypnotist as a sort of Svengali who wears a black gown and waves his hands. Actually, according to one expert in the field of hypnosis, Dr. Theodore X. Barber of the Medfield Foundation in Massachusetts, through careful control of imagery a psychologist can train a person to produce practically any phenomenon that would occur in ordinary hypnosis. As a matter of fact, one can give research subjects and others the identical instructions that would be given in order to hypnotize them, but not use the word "hypnosis," and these individuals won't feel hypnotized but will still be able to produce the same kinds of images and other phenomena that are ordinarily associated with hypnosis.

In other words, the capacity for imagery is one of our latent potentials. The eleven simple exercises in this chapter should help almost everyone to develop this capacity.

Learning
about Yourself
through Daydreams

Daydreams can tell us a great deal about the hidden aspects of our personalities. For instance, someone who sees him or herself as a highly competitive, tough invididual, but whose daydreams are mainly concerned with being tenderly cared for by someone else, might want to reassess his or her goals. Certainly, when a person's daydreams run completely counter to life experiences, that person may be overlooking an important part of his or her essential nature. Let's look at a few examples:

Charles R. is a scientist who spends 16 hours a day in his laboratory. He insists that his deepest wish is to win the Nobel Prize in chemistry, or, if that is not possible, at least a very large research grant from the Rockefeller Foundation. His expectations are not unrealistic. He is a highly gifted researcher with an almost unquenchable drive for hard work. But, with increasing frequency, he has been experiencing periods of deep depression. He can't understand why he is unhappy; his life seems to be going in exactly the direction he had planned and foreseen. He seeks professional help when his depression begins to interfere with his work.

40

Asked whether he has any daydreams except the one in which he is applauded after giving his Nobel Prize speech, he confides to the therapist that he frequently and consistently fantasizes himself as a great lover, the most popular host in town, and the kind of man to whom others turn instinctively when they are in trouble. The few women he has dated (and with whom he discussed Konrad Lorenz's anthropological reservations about the fundamental basis of democracy, or the latest developments in molecular plant biology) would be more than a little amused if he told them of his fantasies. So would his research assistants, who look at him more as a work-oriented ogre than a father confessor. But his daydreams indicate to the therapist, and eventually to him, that he often feels lonely and isolated in his work. He wants and needs to develop relationships with people as well as with cell molecules and the works of Konrad Lorenz. If he continues to ignore these aspects of his inner nature, he may get into serious emotional trouble. His fantasies show that in many ways he is something of a stranger to himself.

Then there is Margaret S., a jolly, overweight mother of four who goes into therapy because of sudden, unexplained anxiety attacks. Although she protests that she is happy in her role as wife and mother, she consistently fantasizes herself as a size-eight model who also happens to be the president of a large corporation. Her daydreams show that, even though she thinks she should be satisfied with her present life, she actually yearns for something else. And, although she may protest that fat is beautiful, her fantasies show that she does not like her body image.

Obviously, neither the scientist nor the homemaker is going to translate these daydreams diectly into real life. Charles will not become the community swinger to the detriment of his research; Margaret will not leave her husband and children to work her way up the corporate ladder in some major industry. But each can modify his **41** or her lifestyle so that it includes some of the ingredients that are now missing. Charles may spend a few hours less at the laboratory and cultivate some social and conversational skills. Margaret may join a weight reduction and exercise class and plan to get her real estate license.

Since the beginning of recorded history, civilizations have placed great importance on the interpretation of night dreams. For instance, the early Egyptians and Babylonians wrote dream books. The Greek Oracles were, of course, based partly on dreams, and Greek legends record the importance of dreams in the lives of heroes and villains. For instance, Oedipus, as a tiny infant, was deposited in the desert to be eaten by wild beasts because his father dreamed that this particular son would bring bad luck to the family. He was destined, according to the dream, to kill the father and marry the mother. Oedipus was rescued by a kindly shepherd and eventually fulfilled the prophecy, much to his father's, his mother's, and his own regret, but certainly to the advantage of tragedy playwrights and enthusiastic psychoanalysts.

In the Bible, Joseph had a series of dreams that seemed to his brothers to be fairly ominous. For instance, he dreamed that he saw one central star (himself) to which all the other stars bowed down. Then he saw a large haystack to which all the smaller haystacks bowed. The brothers were aware of the fact that their father already favored Joseph over all his other sons. Jacob even gave his son a coat of many colors (while the other brothers, sons of Jacob's first, unwanted wife, presumably had to wear drab tan garments). So they tore up Joseph's coat, pushed him into a ditch, and eventually sold him to a nomadic tribe as a slave. They poured a few ounces of animal blood over the coat and told their father that Joseph had been killed by wild animals. Joseph eventually landed in Egypt, where he went right on dreaming. Only this time he turned his awareness of fantasy into

42

a practical direction as an interpreter of others' dreams. Dreams supposedly could predict the future and he made a few interpretations that came true. As a result, he was released and became an important minister in the household of the Egyptian pharaoh.

Night dream analysis seems to be just as important today as it was to the ancient Egyptians, Greeks, and early Jews. Every large paperback book rack is weighed down with dream analysis books, and for those with a deeper interest and more money, psychoanalysis and other forms of psychiatric theory and practice offer opportunities to explore the meaning of night dreams.

Daydreams have not been given nearly as much importance in assessing personality and character. In a way, it's strange they have not. Daydreams are more conscious and more controllable than night dreams, and therefore give strong indications of a person's inner life and potential. They are a much neglected source of information, particularly since they are usually more accessible than night dreams. It's often hard to remember what we dreamed while we were sleeping, but, with some training and experience, we can usually remember our waking fantasies.

Why are both night dreams and daydreams important? Partly because they reveal a great deal about the material that our brain stores away. A surprising amount of what has happened to us, what we have seen and what we have felt, is stored away in our brain. What we choose to recall, what we mull over and recreate, tells us what we have found important, pleasurable, or perhaps hurtful and frightening. If we keep a record of our night dreams and daydreams, we will usually be able to trace a pattern of joy and unhappiness, delight and fear, desire and aversion. By keeping such a record, we eventually will be able to tell a great deal about ourselves, and we may decide to change or modify some aspects of our lives which have been illuminated for us.

43

Because daydreams are more controllable than night dreams, some people tend to worry about them unduly. They will stop themselves when they find that they have aggressive, angry, or graphic sexual fantasies, for instance. It's important to understand that there is a vital difference between dreams (day or night) and real life. If among your many fantasies you have persistent daydreams about throttling your boss, this does not mean that you are a potential murderer. It only means that you are having some problems about the boss and that perhaps you should think about changing jobs or trying to correct the difficulties between the two of you. If you dream of making passionate love to a movie star or a friend, this does not mean that you are being unfaithful, or even *wish* to be unfaithful, to your wife or husband. In spite of what the Bible says, at least one president of the United States seems to believe that lusting in one's heart does not equal adultery. It just means that you have an active fantasy life. So, there's no cause to feel guilty about your night or day fantasy life. What goes on in your head is your own business, unless, of course, you wish to tell it to a psychiatrist or a *Playboy* interviewer.

Laboratory research has proven that we experience periods of so-called "dreaming sleep" or REM (Rapid Eye Movement) sleep periodically throughout the night. (Exactly why our eyes should be moving around while we dream has not yet been precisely established by researchers, although some have proposed that we may be scanning the dream scene.) However, we may not remember everything that we dreamed at night. We tend to recall dreams that occur just before we awaken; but even those dreams can be forgotten quickly once we are thoroughly aroused and have become involved in the activities of the day. Therefore, if you are truly interested in keeping track of night dreams, you might want to write them down as

44

soon as possible after waking up. A small stack of 3-by-5 cards or a notebook kept on your bedside table will serve as a good record-keeping device.

As we have said, daydreams are more consciously controllable than night dreams. They can be turned on and off at will. They can also be replayed, sometimes in full stereophonic sound and glowing technicolor, like a videotape. So it's not as important to write them down immediately. But if you regularly set aside short periods of time to write down your daydreams, you will be able to collect an accurate record. A useful technique again may be to carry a pad and during idle moments of a day—at a bus stop, on the train, during a coffee break—try to recall a few fantasies or write down what you've just been thinking.

Most people won't, of course, want to record every dream and every fantasy. But anyone who spends a month keeping track of a dozen or so dreams and a few days' worth of fantasies may be able to spot a trend running through them, all of which may provide valuable clues to unsuspected aspects of personality and hidden feelings.

In trying to understand what a dream means, you may want to look at certain specific attributes of it. For instance, are some scenes and themes repeated? If they are, they may reveal to you areas of your personality you had not previously known. There are several criteria which can help you decide how important the material in the daydream or night dream is to you. You can score yourself from 1 to 5 on the following dream characteristics:

SCORING YOUR DREAMS

1. Is your dream or fantasy purely visual? In other words, when you look back on it does it seem like a silent movie without subtitles? Or do your other senses come into play? For instance, let's assume you were fantasizing about a banquet at which you were the guest of honor. Did you hear the main speaker sing your praises? Did you smell

45

the food? Did you taste the tender and luscious roast beef? Many daydreams consist entirely of conversations you conduct with one or more persons. They might be described as interior dialogues. Did you see the person with whom you were talking? Did you listen to his or her answers and comments? If, in your daydreams, you are always the only talker, you might ask yourself if that's a clue to your real-life behavior. If one sense was involved, score 1. If more than one sense was involved, score higher, up to 5 for especially vivid sensual dreams. Remember, though, that this is not an examination. You are not competing for high points; you just want to learn something about yourself.

Interestingly enough, we can "see" scenes, persons, and events in our fantasies that we have never seen in real life. Research with children who were born blind has revealed that even someone who has never experienced sight may still have a fantasy life full of sounds, tastes, smells, the sensations of touch, or the feeling of motion.

2. Are your dreams personal or impersonal? let's assume you are dreaming about a bank robbery. Are you a spectator, watching events as if they were on the CBS Evening News? Are you actively involved, either as one of the perpetrators or as a victim? Or do you switch back and forth between roles? If the dream seemed very personal to you, score 5. If you were an indifferent bystander, score 1. Other degrees of involvement will be scored from 2 to 4.

3. Was the dream (day or night) relevant to your real life? If you daydream about visiting the harem of an Arabian sheik, you are probably just seeking a perfectly legitimate escape from everyday problems. On the other hand, if you daydream about asking your boss for a raise, you are dealing in an aspect of your life that is quite relevant. You may even be rehearsing a conversation you plan to have sometime in the near future. Score

1 to 5, with 5 representing extreme, obvious relevance to your current life situation.

4. How vivid was your dream? Did you seem to be looking at a world through a thick fog, or was everything clear and sharp? Did you see events in color or in black and white? Could you hear clearly what was being said? Score from 1 to 5, with higher scores representing the more vivid experiences. By averaging your ratings for a whole series of dreams along the dimensions of 1) range of senses, 2) personal relevance, 3) significance to daily life, and 4) vividness, you can get a sense of how high you rate on each and how intense your dream life is on an overall basis when you add all the scores.

You may want to score day and night dreams on separate scales, since daydreams are apt to be less vivid than night dreams.

If you find a consistent pattern in your day and night dreams, you may be able to see clearly what major human drives move you most. Your fantasies also might provide important clues to what it is you really want, or for that matter, don't want. First consider what themes crop up. To what extent do your fantasies reflect achievement, for instance? If you have not been getting on in your career and have told yourself that this does not matter, while all your day and night dreams show you as overcoming incredible obstacles to reach career peaks, you may have misjudged your own deepest wishes.

HOW TO INTERPRET WHAT YOUR FANTASIES MEAN

If, on the other hand, your fantasies point to passionate, tender love affairs, or deep abiding friendships, while in your everyday life you have been concentrating almost exclusively on career success, something may be telling you that you are suppressing a deep need for giving and receiving affection.

47

To what extent is there a great deal of sexual involvement in your dreams?

Some people spend a great deal of time fantasizing about what psychologists call "harm avoidance." The dreamer calls up incidents involving escapes from dangerous situations, or anticipates various types of unpleasantness that have not occurred yet and dreams up ways to avoid them. We now know that people who watch a great deal of television, say 20 hours or more a week, are more likely to have fantasies of being the victims of violence than are people who watch very little TV.

How important a part does power play in your fantasies? In your day or night dreams do you picture situations in which you can control others, or in which others, with or without your consent, control you?

How important is dependency? How often do you fantasize about having someone care for you, cater to you, and generally devote time and effort to making you happy and comfortable? Do you fantasize about caring for someone else in a similar manner?

There are other human motives that may show up in day and night dreams. When you realize that they are important to you, you will probably recognize them.

Now look at your scores for the particular types of content that show prominence, e.g., dependency, power, sexual involvement. How often does one or more of these themes arise? If you are keeping track, you will probably find that you will be able to trace three or more important elements. If you compare the elements of your fantasy life with those in your real life, you may learn a lesson about yourself: if your dreams and your real-life goals and efforts coincide, you've probably instinctively been doing what is right for you all along. If they don't, you may

48 have been hiding certain important motives and

drives from yourself and may wish to reevaluate your life efforts.

Some daydream patterns may well be signals that something in one's life is not right and that professional help may be needed. Researchers in the field, such as J. L. Singer and John Antrobus, among others, have identified three definite patterns of daydreaming:

CAN DAYDREAMS SERVE AS DANGER SIGNALS?

1. The *positive, vivid daydreams,* consist of what we might call wishful thinking: imagining pleasant vacations, winning the state lottery, a conversation with our favorite actor or author, or being nominated for the National Book Award. This kind of daydreaming is obviously fun and will help to relax us and make us feel happier and better about ourselves. Of course, someone who spends time daydreaming of, for example, inheriting a huge sum of money, to the extent that his or her job is neglected, might get fired. Daydreams are like every other aspect of life: they become harmful if they are used to escape from necessary occupations.

2. Another pattern of daydreaming, called guilty or dysphoric, is mainly unpleasantly tinged or toned. We've all had guilty daydreams occasionally. You may have been rude to a friend and imagine this friend being really downcast by your behavior. Or you may have decided to visit someone in the country for Thanksgiving even though your mother expects you to have dinner with her. You can then imagine Mom looking at the huge, uneaten turkey, weeping into her apron. This kind of guilty daydream can make us miserable. So can fantasies of anger and hostility—getting revenge on people who have offended us, for instance. Sometimes such fantasies are healthy, even though they make us feel a little guilty. After all, it's preferable to daydream of annihilating a competitor or of punching the boss than to carry out such as act. And, as we

49

mentioned before, what goes on in your head usually does not harm another person. However, if you spend most of your time in this kind of unpleasant fantasy, if it becomes the predominant pattern of your inner life, some kind of professional help is probably indicated.

3. The third type of daydreaming pattern reflects a kind of *mind-wandering* in which our thoughts don't seem to be able to settle down on one particular aspect of life. You may ask yourself what it was that you were thinking about. You just don't seem to be able to get a handle on your thoughts. All of us do this occasionally, but if you spend a great deal of time in this type of mind-wandering, and especially if you feel angry or depressed as a result of it, something may be wrong. People who show a consistent pattern of this kind of thought may also show other signs of emotional disturbance. It might be worthwhile for such a person to check out his or her emotional health with a professional.

There is one additional danger in this kind of dream or daydream analysis. Many of us are enthusiastic amateur psychoanalysts. The most obscure and obtuse psychological theories have become part of the mainstream of American thought. Mental health professionals of every persuasion write in magazines, produce books (like this one), and appear on TV talk shows. It's a great temptation to use some of this theory to try to interpret our fantasy life. That's probably not a good idea. Human emotions are not as simply analyzed and treated as one might think from listening to the latest exponent of a school of popular psychology on the Johnny Carson show. So, in interpreting what you dream and daydream, you will probably learn most by considering your dream scene to be exactly what it seems. Trying to use complicated symbolic interpretations may make good party conversation, but can also lead you up all kinds of irrational garden paths.

50

At a recent psychiatric conference, a speaker was expounding on symbol interpretations. This particular gentleman tended to see almost everything as a phallic symbol. At the close of the meeting, while everybody was still applauding, another psychiatrist got up and announced, disgustedly: "A telephone pole is a telephone pole is a telephone pole!" Then he left the room. Freud himself once said that in a dream, "A cigar is sometimes just a cigar!" You might heed this warning when you attempt to interpret your own fantasy material.

Relaxation without Pills or Alcohol

The airplane is going through what the captain calls "extreme areas of air turbulence." Everybody, including even the cabin attendants, are pulling their seat belts tighter, clutching the arms of their seats, and holding their breaths, while the plane bounces around like a Ping-Pong ball. Joe Smith, sitting in the back of the plane, is sleeping peacefully.

Top management of a large company has just announced a complete reorganization affecting the entire executive staff. Nobody is sure whether he or she is going to be promoted or fired. In the executive lunchroom, food remains untouched on plates, but there is an abnormal demand for double Scotches on the rocks. Several men who gave up smoking some time ago are apologetically borrowing cigarettes from tablemates. Lenore Jenkins, Vice-President of Marketing, calmly orders a second helping of salad to go with her iced tea.

The office of the oral surgeon is crowded. Many of the patients have been waiting for at least an hour. There has been an unexpected emergency, the nurse has informed them. She didn't

54

give out any additional information. The scene is one of barely contained anxiety and tension. Everyone looks as if he or she would like to be almost any other place. People are shifting back and forth in their chairs, coughing nervously and rattling magazines and newspapers. Althea Brown, relaxed and seemingly quite happy, is looking over some travel brochures about the Fiji Islands that were left in the waiting room by another patient. She actually seems to be enjoying herself.

There are some people who apparently can relax at will, even in the most tension-provoking circumstances. Most of us can't. However, we can train ourselves to deal more comfortably with tension and anxiety.

There are a number of helpful relaxation exercises that have been worked out by psychiatrists and psychologists. All involve a conscious ability to relax the body combined with specific repeated phrases or preplanned daydreams. We will explain two of the more effective relaxation techniques at the end of this chapter.

First, though, it will help if you try to pinpoint exactly what is making you tense. The airline passengers, company executives, and oral surgery patients, of course, knew exactly what was bothering them. They were all suffering from a bad case of anticipatory anxiety. There are times, however, when many of us just feel tense and anxious without being quite sure why we feel so upset.

You probably know what's happening in your body. When your emotions flash danger signals to your glands, unneeded adrenaline pours through your system. If you are then attacked by a mugger or are facing a neighbor's snarling German Shepherd, the adrenaline will be very useful in helping you to fight or flee. But in situations where the danger is not as obvious, you may just sit there, your muscles getting tighter, your head throbbing, and your heart beating faster, waiting for the worst (whatever that may be) to happen.

It's helpful to know that there are other **55**

emotional states besides fear that can arouse you or create body stress. For instance, there's boredom. Waiting for a commuter train that's 45 minutes late, watching an intensely uninteresting movie (that your companion for some inexplicable reason enjoys), or typing up a manuscript of the history of the Japanese Navy before World War I (with ten footnotes on every page) can produce symptoms of anxiety and tension very similar to those we feel when we are in true physical danger.

You can also feel tense if you are annoyed or angry with no outlet for your irritation. Sitting in an office reception area waiting for an appointment that was scheduled 30 minutes ago, for instance, can cause all kinds of tension. So can an employer who wants to discuss, in great detail, Jimmy Carter's latest appointments, the current heat wave, the results of a public opinion poll on tax reform, or his or her own pet theories on water fluoridation—anything and everything but that raise you requested and which you assumed was to be the topic of this conversation. So can a plumber who takes one look at a dripping faucet and says, "You've got trouble, lady," and then spends the next hour apparently just hitting the pipes and muttering to himself. You can't scold the receptionist, yell at the boss, or fire the plumber. So you feel tense and anxious instead. But if you clearly understand what's bothering you, it's often easier to allow yourself to relax and drift with the tide. After all, you can't change the situation, so you might as well wait it out in as much comfort as possible.

Ordering yourself to relax, and then using your willpower to make a conscious effort to do so, will almost always be self-defeating. Furthermore, if you cannot will yourself to relax, you have failed to deal with your discomfort in a way you intellectually know to be reasonable and practical. So you have added to the existing tension an overlay of self-blame or even guilt, and you now feel even more tense.

56

The relaxation techniques we are recommending, when combined with appropriate daydreams, will work as well as if not better than a pill or a double Scotch. A pill or drink might sometimes work faster or take less effort, but each external substance you pour into your body has its own, often potentially harmful, consequences.

Throughout the ages, physicians and philosophers have developed structured methods of progressive relaxation. Yoga is obviously such a method. So is transcendental meditation. So are biofeedback exercises. So, for that matter, are certain kinds of prayer. Psychologists have adapted these methods to help their patients feel calm and peaceful enough to deal with their problems. The following two methods work well for most people. One requires an appropriate setting, such as a bedroom or living room, and about half an hour of free time. The other takes less time and can be used almost anywhere (although not while driving on an ice-coated highway or during important business negotiations). You might want to try both methods to find the one that suits you best.

METHOD I*

1. Lean back in a comfortable chair. Put your feet up, if possible, and shut your eyes. Try to let tension flow from your body.

2. Take a deep breath and hold it for about five seconds. (Don't bother to time yourself with a stopwatch. That would be counterproductive. Just estimate.)

3. Exhale naturally and slowly through your nose and say a phrase like "one." You'll notice that you feel calmer already.

4. Breathe normally and concentrate on feeling

*Modified from the Jacobsen Progressive Relaxation Method and the biofeedback research of Herbert Benson and his collaborators at Harvard. Based on Edmund Jacobsen, *Progressive Relaxation* (Chicago: University of Chicago Press, 1938), Copyright © 1929, ·1938 by the University of Chicago Press. Reprinted with permission.

relaxed all over. Your limbs feel heavy, your muscles loose.

5. Concentrate on this pleasant feeling and learn to enjoy it.

6. After about a minute, start to teach yourself the difference between tension and relaxation. Try to tense every muscle in your body: your toes, your calves, your thighs, your stomach, your hands, your arms, your chest, your back. Feel the tension all over your body, getting tighter and tighter.

7. Now let go, and relax again muscle by muscle. Concentrate on how calm and relaxed you feel. Let your thoughts "touch" each body area as it relaxes after being tensed.

8. Close your eyes. Feel how much more relaxed you can become with your eyes closed. Open them again and notice the difference.

9. Keep your eyes closed and take a very deep breath. Hold it. Relax your body. You will notice tensions from holding your breath. Now let your breath out through your nose, and feel the deepening relaxation. Breathe normally and allow relaxation to flow into every part of your body. Your arms and legs will feel heavy as if it would take a special effort to move them. You may feel warm. You may also feel a tingling sensation in your hands, your feet, or some other part of your body.

10. Keep on relaxing more every time you exhale. Think of the word "relax" or "one" or "om!" as you breathe out. You are feeling very tranquil and serene.

11. Deepen the relaxation by thinking of or softly saying more peace-inducing words: "calm," "happy," "sleepy," for instance, as you breathe out.

12. Count backwards from 10 to 1. At the count of 5, open your eyes. At the count of 1, stretch and yawn. Notice how calm you feel. Enjoy that

feeling.

13. Close your eyes again. Picture a beautiful, peaceful scene. You may be able to remember such a scene from your past: a running brook, a waterfall, a snow-covered hillside, or a colorful sunset. Paint that picture in your mind and put yourself in it. Listen to the sounds: birds singing, water running, etc., as well as seeing the picture. Stay there for several minutes. Besides feeling relaxed, you may also begin to feel happy or contented.

14. Open your eyes, get up slowly, stretch, and tackle whatever it was that made you tense or anxious in the first place.

METHOD II

This system takes less time and does not require as much privacy as Method I. You might feel a little conspicuous if you sat leaning back in your office chair or in a waiting room, with your feet up and your eyes closed, for half an hour at a time—and the embarrassing questions you would be asked about your strange behavior would certainly not enhance relaxation.

1. Get comfortable. Leaning back in a chair with your feet up may be best. If that's not possible, just relax as much as you can wherever you happen to be.

2. Breathe in slowly through your nose, then breathe out. Do this about ten times while loosening your tense muscles as much as you can. Close your eyes.

3. As you breathe out, say "relax" or "calm" to yourself. (Those who are familiar with Oriental meditation techniques may recognize this method. The words "relax" and "calm" function in similar ways to mantras like "ommm" or "homm." There's nothing magical about a mantra. It's merely a sound that comes fairly naturally as one breathes out.)

4. Keep doing this for about two minutes, then

59

switch to a beautiful, peaceful scene. Keep yourself there until you can feel all the tension going out of your body.

5. Get up, stretch, tense and then loosen some of your muscles. You'll probably feel just fine.

Here are some additional suggestions:

1. If you've never tried programmed relaxation techniques combined with mind images to combat tension and stress, Method I may work best for you. After you've mastered the more complicated, time-consuming methods, try the simple ones. Learning how to use daydreams to diminish stress takes practice, just as acquiring any other type of skill does.

2. The best time to practice relaxation techniques is when you are *not* under stress. You can make a pleasant game out of your practice sessions. You might want to try relaxation plus mind trips the first time just before going to bed. They are an excellent weapon against insomnia, too.

3. You may find that when you are already somewhat relaxed you can slip in and out of daydreams easily, using almost no programmed relaxation system, but that the technique does not seem to work under stressful conditions. Realize that you may have to use a more time-consuming method when you are especially tense. And don't worry about your seeming inability to relax. Worry and tension just feed on each other. Don't try to *force* yourself to relax; it won't work. Just do the exercises, taking as much time as you need. In almost all cases, you'll feel more comfortable after a while.

4. Some people seem to have trouble picking out the lovely, peaceful nature scene to which they want to transport themselves in their minds. Most people can remember a time in their lives when they looked out of a window at snow falling or
60 sat in a meadow and watched the clouds, agreeing

with poet Robert Browning that "God's in his heaven, all's right with the world." If you can recall the scene in your mind, you usually can also recall the feeling. It's also possible, of course, to have several pleasant places into which your imagination can take you. Some people have found that they can vary their destinations with the seasons. For instance, on a broiling hot summer day they picture themselves sitting in a meadow by a brook, looking at a snow-covered mountain; on the other hand, on a cold and stormy day a short stay on a sun-drenched, white beach looking out at a clear blue ocean with sailboats on the horizon might be pleasant. That's one of the greatest advantages of this kind of mind traveling. One can go wherever one wants—and without even having to worry about the weather.

So, if the first imaginary scene does not work, try another one. And don't try to think them up when you're already tense. It's better to develop a number of such vivid fantasies when you're relaxed, then hold them in reserve for the times you need to call on them to reduce stress.

5. When you are particularly tense and worried, the everyday world may begin to intrude on your imaginary scene. If just pushing the worrisome problem aside and concentrating on the scene does not work, it may be necessary to start again the whole procedure of first relaxing and then using the daydream. Particularly if you have not yet had a great deal of practice in relaxation plus mind images, repeating the procedures several times may be necessary before you can achieve a calm and relaxed state of mind.

6. There are any number of commercial cassette tapes, advertised in various magazines, that are supposed to help with relaxation and mind trips. Some cost as much as $35 a set. The tapes instruct the buyer to go through exercises similar to the ones we are recommending. If you really would enjoy being urged on by a well-modulated, smooth **61**

voice and you feel that you can afford the price, the tapes will certainly do no harm and may even be helpful. On the other hand, you can make your own tape. Have a friend who reads well and is endowed with mellow-sounding vocal cords read the instructions slowly and calmly. You will need a cassette recorder-player for the commercial tapes in any case. Blank cassettes can be bought for 98 cents. It's worth a try before you spend a larger sum on the commercially recorded cassettes. But probably you can rely as much on your own imagination and won't really require tapes at all.

An important principle to keep in mind in using imagery to reduce tension is that of *specificity*. Formula phrases such as "I can relax!" or "I can be peaceful," or even prayers or mantras that are repeated automatically usually don't work over the long run. Theodore X. Barber, whose work has enhanced our understanding of the mysteries of hypnosis, has carried out important studies with his colleagues at the Medfield foundation in Massachusetts that point to the importance of vivid, specific, *goal-directed* fantasies. If you want to experience a bodily change or movement, you must imagine a very specific fantasy that can bring that change about. Merely saying "think positively" or "take it easy, now" is not sufficient; in your mind's eye you must develop an imaginary *context,* a vivid environment in which your body actually could relax. Some people are more relaxed by the seashore, others by mountains or woods; some might picture their easy chair at home, others might visualize being in the arms of a loved one. Somebody else's fantasy or catch phrase won't work for you unless it ties in directly with your own memories and fantasies.

A young woman we know was undergoing relaxation exercises with a therapist as a preliminary to trying to overcome a strong irrational fear (see Chapter 6). The therapist suggested a scene she might imagine: "You're sitting by a lake. It's quiet, you can hear only the soft ripples against the sides of some rocks and the chirping of birds."

"Shut up and let me do this myself," responded our friend. She had been picturing a scene in the mountains during winter—a cross-country ski trail through pine woods, everything white or silent with only the greenery above and the scent of the pines. Since she came from a mountain state background, such scenes were the ones most vividly linked to peace in her mind. In directing her thoughts vividly into such a scene, she experienced in mind and muscle the same dropping away of stress that she had often experienced in her childhood.

Once you have practiced the relaxation plus daydream technique to deal with stress and tension, you will find that you are able to use a similar system of loosening up your muscles and directing your mind into specific channels of imagination to accomplish other tasks: minimizing physical pain, curing yourself of certain irrational fears or aversions, and overcoming bad habits, for instance.

63

Mind Trips
and Phobias

Sylvia Andrews is terrified of flying. She knows perfectly well that according to the best available statistics, she is at least 90 percent safer "flying the friendly skies of United" than driving her Volkswagen on the Pennsylvania Turnpike. But in her heart she's convinced that if people were meant to fly at the speed of sound, half a mile up, someone would have arranged to repeal the law of gravity. So, she takes trains, boats, buses, or her Volkswagen to get to her various destinations. She's a copywriter for a New York advertising agency, spends her vacation in Connecticut, and goes to visit her mother in California on a bus. Thus she is able to avoid planes.

David Swift goes into a panic when confronted with examination papers. He's a very intelligent young man, but he broke out in a cold sweat when he had to answer ten simple questions on an examination for a driver's license. His thoughtful parents arranged for him to go to a progressive private school where no exams were given, and an equally progressive college. He's done very well and has been able to avoid competitive situations that cause him intense discomfort.

Herbert Brown is terrified of going to a dentist. He knows that his teeth are in very bad shape. He also knows that his 6-year-old son goes to see the dentist regularly, twice a year, and comes out of the examining room smiling happily. Nevertheless, every time Herbert thinks of having a cavity filled, he pictures a fiend similar to the one played by Laurence Olivier in the movie *Marathon Man*. The scene in that film in which the character played by Olivier uses a dental drill to torture information out of hapless Dustin Hoffman confirms Herbert's worst nightmares about visits to the dentist's office. So Herbert has given up ice-cold drinks, peanut butter, and a few other items of food and drink that make his teeth hurt, while he continues to postpone making that much-needed dental appointment.

Shirley Edwards is terrified of driving a car. She lives in a suburban area, about 10 miles from the nearest source of public transportation, and the Edwards family is the only one in the neighborhood that owns only one car—the one that Don Edwards drives to work every morning.

Friends and neighbors are convinced that Shirley's insistence on not driving is somehow motivated by an intense idealism: she is a dedicated energy conserver, they feel, or a clean-air advocate. At any rate, they are very cooperative about driving her to the supermarket or to school board meetings when Don and the family car are unavailable. Don, of course, knows that Shirley's avoidance of driving has nothing to do with idealism, and so does she. But with good planning and image building she has managed to get herself chauffeured wherever she needs to go.

All four of these people suffer from a fairly common psychiatric disability: a phobia. Among the most common phobias are: fear of heights, fear of closed-in spaces, fear of open spaces, fear of competitive situations (such as examinations), fear of animals (especially snakes, spiders, mice, rats, cats, and dogs), fear of dentists or physicians, and fear of blood. Sometimes two or more phobias combine to produce yet a third phobia. For instance, Sylvia Andrews may be afraid of heights and of closed-in spaces, thus producing her problem with airplanes. A similar combination of phobias might produce a fear of escalators or elevators. Fear of machinery plus fear of open spaces (agoraphobia) might produce Shirley Edwards's driving jitters.

Most people find that having such a phobia is a little annoying, but they are rarely motivated enough to seek help unless their fear begins to interfere seriously with their daily lives. As a matter of fact, almost all of us have at least some irrational fears that occasionally cause us to behave in foolish ways but which often don't come up enough in our lives to create any serious consequences. If you examine your own beliefs and behavior, you may come upon some minor fear or superstition that you picked up from a teasing relative or babysitter when you were a child or from a scary campfire ghost story. So many of us won't walk under a ladder or feel uncomfortable about having a black cat cross our paths. And we have a whole nation that developed a swimming phobia at the whim of commercial film-makers who terrorized us with a fear of sharks when the evidence was plain that millions of people around the world swim in the sea all the time without ever encountering anything more predatory than a small crab.

Let's take the case of Sylvia Andrews. She sought professional help when she was promoted from copywriter to copy supervisor. Her new job meant that, instead of sitting behind a desk in the New York office, she would be calling on the agency's clients in many parts of the United States. Getting there by bus or train or Volkswagen was just not possible. She would either have to turn down the promotion or get over her irrational fear.

After David Swift got his B.A. at the progressive college, he decided that he wanted to become a lawyer. He quickly learned that every reputable law school in the United States requires applicants to take a standardized legal aptitude test: a five-hour written examination. Also, after he finishes law school, he will have to take a Bar Examination if he wants to practice his profession. Obviously, he too will somehow have to get over his phobia unless he wishes to change his entire life plan.

Herbert Brown finds that he is suffering from a tooth abscess and that no amount of aspirin, even when reinforced with several stiff drinks, will stop the pain. Obviously he needs an emergency appointment with the dentist, and the sooner the better.

Shirley Edwards's husband developed cataracts, which meant that he had to have eye surgery and would not be able to drive the family car for at least two months. For a while at least, she would not be able to count on him as her chauffeur. She now had to take *him* to his medical appointments, the office, and so on. Her driving phobia had become more than a minor inconvenience; it had turned into a serious problem.

We may assume that Sylvia, David, Herbert, and Shirley are now sufficiently motivated to want to overcome their phobias. How can they go about it? Psychiatrists and psychologists use a variety of methods to help patients rid themselves of their irrational and disabling fears. An analytically oriented therapist would probably attempt to help the patient find the root cause of the phobia. When that cause is discovered, presumably the patient would be able to rid him or herself of the fear.

The four individuals in our case histories do not have a great deal of time to get over their fears. They will have to seek a more rapid form of therapy than analysis. So there are two possibilities open to them. They can look for a therapist who will attempt to eliminate their phobias quickly, without necessarily looking for the root causes, or **69** they can try to cure themselves. One type of treatment that is often recommended for irrational fears is "behavior therapy," an attempt to change a person's behavior rather than changing his or her basic personality through analysis.

Since the men and women in the case histories need to get over their problems as quickly as possible, behavior therapy might be a good solution for them. This form of therapy is built on setting up fantasies that will place the patient in the situation he or she fears, slowly and methodically, step by step, with the patient always in control of getting out of the situation when the idea becomes too threatening. As the person becomes comfortable with the simulated situation, he or she may well be able to deal with it in reality also.

Let's take Sylvia Andrews and her fear of flying. A therapist would probably first teach her to relax completely. (See relaxation exercises in Chapter 5.) Once she is able to do this easily, she will probably be asked to picture herself going, step by step, through an imaginary flight.

First, she may be asked to imagine herself looking at travel folders about lovely and exotic places which she can reach only by plane. The next steps might be to picture herself walking into a travel agent's office to make arrangements for the trip; picturing herself packing her suitcase, picking out exactly the right clothes; taking the airport bus, checking in at the departure counter, going through airport security, and finally getting on the plane and fastening her seat belt. Eventually, she can imagine herself flying high up in the clouds, looking down at a beautiful, azure ocean or a mountainous landscape, feeling completely relaxed and enjoying a delicious in-flight dinner.

She can go through this procedure step by step, over and over again. As soon as she feels anxious, she will be asked to stop the imaginary flight plan, go back into a completely relaxed state, and start all over again.

Can you cure yourself of an irrational fear? Here are some methods you might try. Let's assume that, like Shirley Edwards, you are afraid of driving a car. (Similar steps would help you in overcoming other kinds of phobias, but driving happens to be a fairly common one.)

First of all, you should try to analyze your fear carefully. Write down everything and anything that might have contributed to your phobia. Were you ever in an accident, even a slight one? If you have driven a car but are now frightened, has anything happened to activate your phobia? Did you almost cause a mishap once that might have hurt you or someone else? Have you recently heard about a bad accident that happened to someone you know? Do you identify in any special way with that person? Did you see a newspaper picture or a television show that featured an automobile accident which particularly frightened you? Analyzing some of the causes of your phobia will help you to set your mind trips to overcome your fears. It's easier to combat known terrors than unknown ones.

Let's assume you have discovered that your fear of driving arises from a deep conviction that, somehow, you will never be able to handle a car safely. Of course, there could be perfectly rational causes for this fear. You may have especially bad eyesight or some other physical handicap that would make it hard for you to become a good driver. In that case, talk over your problem with an expert. People with many kinds of physical handicaps have learned how to drive cars safely by using special equipment and special training.

However, let's assume that your problem is strictly psychological—all physical causes have been eliminated—and that you have driven in the past. Now you can start to work on your specific psychological problem.

First, practice the relaxation exercises in Chapter 5. They are absolutely necessary to the mind scenario you will be using to overcome your

71

fears. Practice them first without even thinking about driving a car, so that you will be able to relax completely the second you feel afraid. Once you have done this, you can start to deal with your specific phobia.

Set up a careful sequence of activities you will be picturing, going from the least frightening aspect to the most frightening. Again, it will help to write down the gradual steps you will be taking in your mind. As you do your mind-trip exercises, you will follow these steps exactly. Here are some of the steps you might take:

1. Imagine that you are looking over your car and checking it for flat tires or other defects with someone whom you like and trust and who knows all about car safety.

2. Imagine yourself being driven by that person around the neighborhood, being taught various methods of controlling the car.

3. As a next step, you might picture having the same person drive, with you as a passenger, on a superhighway at top legal speed.

4. Imagine yourself taking the wheel of a car, perhaps with the same friend beside you.

5. Imagine yourself driving alone, slowly, in a well-known neighborhood.

6. Picture yourself confidently taking the car on a spin along the highway.

Every time you begin to experience each of the scenes above as vividly as if it's happening, shift your thoughts to your peaceful, relaxing imaginary scene. Allow the *feeling* from the peaceful scene to blend in with the images of the driving scene. If you continue to practice faithfully, you should soon be able to get behind the wheel of your car in reality, not just in your daydream exercises.

Of course, once you've mastered your driving phobia, you may also have to take some real-life practical steps to turn yourself into a safe, confident driver if you haven't been practicing driving for a long time. A course at a good driving school, some private lessons with a friend or relative you trust, or help from a professional driving instructor will be necessary before you can take the car on a cross-country trip, or even a trip into the nearest city. Many people who have developed driving phobias were already careful, competent drivers. They find that once the fear of getting into the car and starting it has been eliminated, they function quite well and are soon driving with ease.

The driving phobia involves some fairly concrete negative mind images; after all, almost everyone has seen a car wreck—if not on the highway, then on the front page of the newspaper or a television newscast. But what about something as abstract as examination phobia, the kind David Swift suffered? Can you use the powers of your imagination to combat this kind of abstract aversion as well? Yes, and by very similar techniques.

Let's assume that you have a terror of written or verbal tests and that you know you will have to take them in order to accomplish whatever plan you have for your life. Again, start with a written list and look carefully at the components of your fear. What makes you most afraid? Going into the examination room? Opening the examination book? Reading the first question, which you are almost sure you won't be able to answer? Or do you fear most the results of possible failure? The disappointment of your family, teachers, or friends? Once you've analyzed, in order of importance, what you fear least and what you fear most, you can design your hierarchy of images accordingly and start practicing.

If what you fear most is that moment when you enter the examination room, allow your imagination to get you there slowly by steps. Picture yourself leaving the house in a relaxed manner (you have plenty of time before the test starts). **73**

You might imagine that you have invited a friend to take you to the place where the exam is being given. Perhaps you can picture spending a few minutes with that friend having a cup of hot coffee and a doughnut before you start your trip to the examination hall. Next, picture yourself confidently walking up the stairs to the place where the exam is being given, greeting friends on the way. Open the door to the room, which does not look forbidding at all—and sit down. So far, so good—especially if what you feared most was the initial shock of having to get yourself to the examination in the first place. Again remember to use the relaxed, peaceful scenes you've developed to bring a pleasant mood into each of the exam scenes you will be visualizing.

Now, let's assume that what you feared most was opening the blue book and finding questions you could not possibly answer. In that case, continue your mind trip to after you have opened your examination book. Instead of obscure and difficult questions, you find that the exam deals with material with which you are familiar. You feel that you can easily and comfortably answer all the questions without undue stress. To top off your mind trip, you can picture yourself getting a good grade and having a party to celebrate your success.

Again, if at any time along your imaginary route, you start feeling anxious, stop and go back to your pleasant, relaxing imaginary resting place. Then start all over again on your mind trip. The chances are that in a relatively short time you will be able to overcome your fear at the very *idea* of having to take an examination.

Of course, as in the case of the driving phobia, there are additional practical steps you can take to help yourself become more confident. For instance, copies of examinations similar to the one you will be taking are usually available in your college or high school library or in bookstores. Most experts feel that you cannot cram for an aptitude test, that is, you cannot raise your score by taking similar tests over and over again. But if your problem is not lack of skill but lack of confidence, taking practice tests can be immensely helpful. If you know that speed will be very important to your test results, it will be helpful to take your practice exam under conditions similar to the real exam: use an alarm clock or a small oven timer (available at any hardware or department store) to time your performance. You'll find that with more confidence, you will probably be able to increase your speed. At any rate, you'll lose that panicky feeling that comes to almost everyone (including nonphobic individuals) when confronted with a time-pressure situation.

One technique for dealing with mild phobias that has proven successful in some well-controlled studies may be termed *vicarious modeling* or *observational learning*. Suppose you are afraid of using the telephone. A surprising number of otherwise reasonably well-adjusted individuals find themselves becoming very tense if they have to call up a doctor or speak to their child's teacher on the phone or ask a repairman to come look at the dishwasher. If there is someone you admire—a person who's poised or who handles phone conversations easily—imagine him or her having to make a series of such calls. Begin by relaxing, and then, using a hierarchy of least to most frightening phone situations, slowly picture your model walking to the phone, picking up the receiver, dialing, and then calmly and assuredly saying: "Hello, there. Is this Dr. Smith? This is Mr. Simmons. I've been troubled by a bad cough...." Once you've run through the sequence a few times without experienceing stress, you might begin to picture yourself in each of these situations. It might even be helpful to talk the conversation out loud, in private. It's a good idea to have a little speech prepared in advance; some people get stymied on just whether to say "Hello," "Hi," "Who's this?" or other pat phrases. You may feel phony at first working from a prepared script for your phone calls, but soon it will **75** become quite natural and you'll find the telephone a friend and not a foe.

Another approach that has been shown to be helpful can be called the *imaginary companion* or *letter to a friend* approach. Rita Lee was scheduled to take an automobile trip through Italy with her husband. She became preoccupied with all of the dangers involved. Her psychotherapist suggested that she take him along as an imaginary companion and describe the scenery to him. First she practiced this alone using a hierarchy of scenes from least to most frightening. She'd picture herself driving on the road toward Venice with her husband. Then she'd imagine herself describing the scenery to the therapist, throwing in a few tourist tidbits or comments on history. Before long she could visualize the settings without fear. When the trip actually took place, Rita found she had very few fears. A few times, as on the winding highway near Sorrento, she did start to panic. She then conjured up the picture of her therapist and started a mental conversation telling him about the trip. The description engrossed her and the fear passed. Her husband, who'd always been perturbed by her previous complaints when they were driving, was much relieved to have her sitting calmly by his side. Now he could concentrate better on his driving.

There are, of course, phobias which are not eliminated by the kind of mind trips we are suggesting. Sometimes a phobia is only a symptom of a deep underlying disturbance. In that case, the phobic person probably will need more extensive therapy.

How can you tell the difference? Many experts in the field believe that a person who suffers from unreasonable fears of a number of unrelated objects or events may need psychotherapy. For instance, someone who is afraid not only of snakes, but also of open spaces, examinations, dentists, and thunderstorms may not benefit from a self-help program, or even from specific

behavior therapy. There are so many fears that it

would take years to work on each one. For a few people, as soon as one fear is conquered, one or two others crop up to take its place. Such multiple recurring fears suggest the need for professional help.

Then there is the person who is getting some kind of secondary psychological gain from a phobia. For instance, the woman who insists that she can't learn to drive may find that she is able to avoid many unpleasant chores. She can't do the weekly grocery shopping by herself; she has to enlist her husband or a neighbor who, incidentally, also helps carry heavy packages. She can't go to the PTA meeting alone (and face her son's teacher who may have a few complaints). Someone has to take her. She can't serve as a volunteer for the local United Way drive because she can't get to meetings. Being helpless may, unconsciously, suit her very well. Of course, there are also men who are afraid of driving, and they usually have been able to enlist their wives, secretaries, or business assistants as chauffeurs. As long as everyone cooperates in taking such an individual wherever he wants or needs to go, he is superficially very well off. He doesn't need to own a second or even a first car. He saves automobile repairs, insurance, and other costs. But if the people who have been willing to help him suddenly start to rebel, he's in serious trouble.

But even if the secondary gain from the phobia seems to be, superficially at least, worthwhile, using a phobia in this way has distinct psychological disadvantages. In the first place, it means that the phobic person is almost forced to manipulate others to gain his or her end. That's not very healthy. Also, someone who needs other people to take over relatively simple tasks that the rest of us are able to perform with ease almost always suffers a lowering of self-esteem. Most people just don't enjoy feeling helpless.

So, it's usually worthwhile to try to analyze why secondary gain seems important and why it **77** may not be simpler and healthier to depend on oneself instead of others. The reason may turn out to be quite obvious, and in that case, self-help techniques may work very well. But if the problem is deep-seated and long-standing, additional professional help may be indicated.

Most of us have some minor kinds of phobias that we probably don't even recognize. There are simple situations that just seem to make us uncomfortable. One person may feel that way about paying monthly bills, another about complaining to a plumber or an electrician whose work has been unsatisfactory. Many people feel uncomfortable walking into a crowded room, at a cocktail party, for instance. If we canvass our lives, we are almost bound to discover such relatively minor fears. We can continue to live with them; they don't seriously disturb us. But life would be more pleasant if we managed to overcome them. And, in such instances the self-help mind trips usually work very well. It's just a matter of recognizing the fear and making up an appropriate scenario to overcome it.

In this chapter we have shown you how you can help yourself overcome phobias and other kinds of irrational fears. You can use similar methods to condition yourself away from behavior that you would like to avoid: excessive smoking, drinking, eating a little too much when you are under pressure or feeling blue. More about that in the next chapter.

7

Using Mental Images
to Overcome
Bad Habits

All of us have a few habits we'd like to overcome. They may be fairly harmless, such as nail-biting, clearing our throats before we speak, or refusing to step on a crack in the pavement. Or they may be seriously detrimental to our mental and/or physical health: smoking three packs of cigarettes a day, drinking too much, or using rich, high-cholesterol foods as tranquilizers.

Over the years you may have tried to break some habit, using your will power alone. This may have worked for a time, but eventually you probably reverted to the same old pattern, thus adding a sense of guilt and failure to your discomfort at not being able to control your actions. Techniques developed to overcome phobias (see Chapter 6) can be used to overcome bad habits as well. There is one difference: instead of imagining pleasant, happy scenes, we will use a kind of aversion therapy: dreaming up highly unpleasant or even disgusting images.

Aversion therapy is an important part of medicine and psychiatry. Usually, physical means such as drugs or electric shocks that cause the patient a certain amount of discomfort are used. For instance, some alcoholics have improved through the use of the drug Antabuse. The drug has no effect by itself, but when it's combined with even a tiny amount of alcohol, its effects can be very uncomfortable: the drinker's face flushes, the heart begins to pound, and dizziness and nausea can make the next 30 minutes exceedingly miserable. If a physician decides on Antabuse therapy for a heavy drinker, the patient will always be warned about the effects of the medication. The drinker is given a dose of Antabuse in the physician's presence and then asked to take a jigger or two of his or her favorite alcoholic beverage. Under medical supervision the patient then experiences the extremely unpleasant side effects of the Antabuse-alcohol combination. After the experience has occurred a few times, most drinkers will avoid alcohol like the plague as long as they are on Antabuse. Some alcoholics need the drug as a crutch for the rest of their lives, others become mentally conditioned to expect the unpleasant aftereffect even without taking the medication. Of course, this technique will work only if the drinker really wants to stop getting drunk. It's up to him or her to continue taking the Antabuse as long as it's needed to control this particular bad habit.

Electric shock has been used in the treatment of various kinds of sexual problems that can get a person into serious trouble with the law. In some prisons and rehabilitation centers, child molesters who are seriously motivated to overcome their compulsion have been treated with electric shock aversion therapy. The system works very simply: the offender is shown a picture (usually on a slide film screen) of the kind of child that aroused him sexually in the past. As he looks at the picture, a painful electric shock is given. After a course of this treatment, the offender usually stops feeling the overwhelming attraction to a potential child victim. He has been retrained to feel aversion where formerly he felt pleasure. Some sex **81** offenders actually present themselves for repeat treatments if they feel that their old compulsion is returning because the aversion has been dissipated after a certain amount of time has passed.

Most of us, of course, do not need to undergo such drastic physical aversion therapy. We can use our minds and imaginations to obtain similar results.

Let's take the chronic nail-biter, for instance. The chances are that he or she will have already tried any number of techniques. If the nail-biting started in childhood, parents may have used a reward and punishment system in an attempt to help the youngster overcome this unattractive and unsanitary habit. Some kind of bitter, evil-tasting liquid may have been painted on the nails. Evidence of renewed nail-biting may have been punished with withdrawal of certain privileges ("You won't be able to go to the movies until those nails show some improvement"). Or evidence of nail growth may have been suitably rewarded ("Now that your nails look so nice, you can have a manicure at the beauty salon" or "Since you seem to have made such a great effort, you may go to see that Roy Rogers movie at the Bijou"). If nails are still being bitten after the child has become an adult, obviously none of this has worked.

If you are a nail-biter, you have nothing to lose and a lot to gain by attempting to overcome the bad habit with mental aversion therapy. This is how you might go about it:

1. Look at your hands.

2. Imagine that your fingers and nails look considerably more revolting than they actually do. For instance, you have bitten your nails way down to the quick and your fingers look bloody and raw. You are then asked to plunge them into salt water.

3. Imagine that your fingers are beginning to ooze a slimy, yellow-green pus that soap and water
can't remove.

4. Picture yourself trying to get rid of this mess by biting your nails even further. The taste is abominable, much worse than the iodine your mother used to put on your nails to keep you from biting them.

5. Keep on chewing on those oozing, slimy nails until you actually gag.

6. Do this regularly, even when you are *not* tempted to bite your nails. Often you will not even be conscious of *when* the nail-biting occurs.

7. If you keep using this kind of mental aversion therapy, you may find that the revolting picture comes to your mind if you just get your fingers near your mouth. That's obviously the beginning of a nail-biting cure.

8. If you find that your old habit has returned after several weeks or months, do the mind exercises again. If they don't work, try to figure out a new and even more revolting picture. Use your imagination. You're bound to come up with something that really makes your stomach turn.

9. Again, look at your hands and allow your mind to produce the disgusting picture even when you are not tempted to put your fingers in your mouth.

10. Eventually, you may find that you have simply broken the habit. You won't need to use the mental aversion technique any longer.

Incidentally, some people are concerned that developing such aversive images about their fingers will be so effective that they won't dare even look at them. They worry that the treatment suggested could lead to people's neglecting to cut their nails at all, allowing their fingers to become claw-like and filthy. Clinical experience and experimental research indicate that such negative consequences of aversive imagery therapy simply don't occur. The goal-directed images help us set in motion acts that are themselves specific and they don't generalize automatically. Instead we find that the procedure helps us to change our attitude toward our behavior. We realize that we *can* control ourselves, and this boost in our sense of self-esteem and competence allows us to look more realistically at what once seemed a frightening situation. The odds are that once you've gained control over a simple bad habit you will review the situation in a more rational and detached fashion.

Obviously, similar techniques can be used to combat smoking and drinking.

Here are a few suggestions for "aversion pictures" for the chronic smoker. This method will work for persons who like to light up during periods of relaxation—after dinner, as part of a social situation. Persons who are addictive smokers, who desperately need a cigarette, who smoke constantly to relieve any kind of psychological stress or discomfort, may need more extensive professional help.

1. Imagine that cigarette smoke is getting into your lungs and corroding them until they are a mass of raw flesh, black pus, and dead tissue. (Actually, that's pretty close to what can happen to your lungs if you continue smoking three packs a day indefinitely.)

2. Look at the cigarette and imagine it's a filthy, dirty stick you picked up on the road. The stick is covered with worms and slime. You are putting it in your mouth and it makes you gag.

3. You are in a room that's airless, hot, and filled with clouds of thick, corrosive smoke. You can hardly breathe. You try to open a window, but it's stuck. You try to open a door, but it's locked. You just have to stay in that room and breathe in the noxious fumes until your head spins.

4. You may want to use just one of these mind pictures (the one that works best) or switch back and forth. Whatever works is right.

84 Or, let's suppose you are worried about becoming a

heavy drinker. A person who is a real alcoholic should seek medical and/or psychological help, incidentally. Chronic alcoholism is very difficult to treat, and this kind of self-help program probably won't work by itself, although it might well be used as an adjunct to other forms of therapy.

But you are the man or the woman who stops at the friendly neighborhood bar for a couple of beers. You find that you are drinking three or four beers followed by a shot or two of hard liquor. You think the time has come to cut it out, but you find that the habit, once established, is hard to break. So the next time you go into the bar, order one beer. Then put your imagination to work.

1. Imagine that someone has just vomited all over your beer glass. Allow your imagination to get as graphic as possible. (Remembering the child in *The Exorcist* who spewed green vomit all over the priest may be exactly what you need.)

2. Now imagine that you are still forced to drink the beer. Do so, and feel the slimy, vile vomit in your mouth.

3. By this time you may feel good and sick. But that's exactly the point. Eventually, you won't even need the mind images; just the sight of a glass of beer may make you feel queasy. At that point, you've broken your habit.

4. If the habit returns, start all over again.

Some people find that they can break bad habits more easily if they imagine someone else in a highly uncomfortable situation, with themselves as unwilling spectators. There is recent research evidence that some people actually do better imagining someone else experiencing pain than imagining themselves in the same situation.

For instance, patients in smoking clinics have been taught to picture, as vividly as possible, a good friend reaching for a cigarette. As soon as he or she lights up, there is a violent electric shock. **85**

The patient can see, in his mind's eye, the friend's hand draw back quickly, and the look of agony on his or her face. Every time the imaginary person touches a cigarette, he or she begins to writhe with pain. This technique is called *vicarious modeling.* It seems to have an especially strong effect on those empathic individuals who tend to feel someone else's pain strongly in real-life situations.

You might want to try using vicarious modeling techniques as well as picturing your own painful experiences. You will probably continue to use whichever method works best for you. Or you may want to switch back and forth between methods, using one to reinforce the other.

Psychologists Frances Stern and Ruth Hoch have used fantasy to help chronically overweight individuals reduce effectively and permanently. They describe their method as "mind trips and constructive daydreaming to unlock your trim self, stop overeating, be more assertive, and like yourself better." The mental images they describe feature such interesting items as talking stuffed cabbage, anti-obesity fortune cookies, and T-shirts with messages on the front and back. Their own message is that most diets don't work (if they did, there would not be a new one every month) unless the fat person undergoes a psychological change and no longer feels compelled to overeat. We agree.

Aversion techniques are sometimes useful when they are used by a therapist in conjunction with psychotherapy and other methods to treat complex emotional problems.

One special case comes to mind. A young woman studying for a college teaching career frequently felt a compulsion to shoplift—to take minor items such as scarves, costume jewelry, or lipsticks from store counters and to walk out the door with them. She had no use for the merchandise she took. In fact, when she got it home, she quickly disposed of it in the nearest trash bin. But she seemed unable to stop herself from sneaking them into her purse or coat pocket at every opportunity.

The young woman was intelligent and sensitive. She realized that she was putting her chosen lifestyle and career in jeopardy; teachers who are arrested for stealing generally have a hard time finding jobs. Also, she had a strong conscience and felt that she had a long-standing, deep-rooted emotional problem which had to be overcome through psychotherapy. But most important, she had to get rid of her immediate behavior pattern before it got her into serious trouble.

Treatment was, of course, aimed at getting at the cause of her problem. But her own priorities were respected. First she was helped, through imagery and imagination, to overcome her need to shoplift.

Every time she felt tempted to pick up an item from a counter, she was instructed to imagine that the item was filthy and repulsive, covered with dirt, slime, germs, and bugs. Usually this image alone proved to be strong enough to help her resist her impulse. If it had not worked, several other scenarios might have been suggested. For instance, she could have imagined herself being arrested while her pocketbook was filled with pilfered merchandise. A mental trip through the arrest procedure, the police lineup, the fingerprinting and court hearing, complete with an indignant scolding by the judge and the shocked silence of her parents and friends, might have been even more of a deterrent than those horribly filthy scarves and lipsticks. In aversion therapy, the most uncomfortable, horrifying, embarrassing, and disgusting mental pictures will probably work best, as opposed to the pleasant scenes and pictures employed in therapy designed to overcome phobias (see Chapter 6).

One might ask whether repeated mind trips into highly unpleasant territories would not eventually depress or otherwise seriously disturb a person. Experienced therapists who have used this technique feel that the opposite tends to be true. Most people become depressed when they feel themselves to be helpless. Dr. Martin Seligman, a researcher at the University of Pennsylvania, has **87** developed a theory that depression can often result from what he calls "learned helplessness": the patient so afflicted has been trained since early childhood to react to a challenge with passivity. Sometimes there may even be some practical gains from this condition, if someone else takes over the task with which the patient apparently could not cope. But the end result of such an attitude is almost always a decrease in self-esteem, which can certainly lead to depression.

Men and women who have learned to cope with bad habits obviously no longer feel like helpless victims governed by their impulses. They know that they can control their behavior with a series of coping techniques they have mastered. This accomplishment will often lead to increased self-esteem and elation, rather than sadness.

If, even after having overcome a destructive habit, you need an additional psychological boost, you can imagine yourself in a situation in which you receive praise and appreciation for your new strength. For instance, it's possible for the nail-biter to picture a scene in which an attractive member of the opposite sex (Catherine Deneuve or Robert Redford) takes his or her hand and remarks on how beautiful it is. The new nonsmoker can imagine that he or she had been invited to lecture on the benefits of clean air to an audience at Harvard Medical School with Dr. Jonas Salk sitting in the front row applauding enthusiastically. Newly cured patients can use their minds to place themselves in any rewarding situation that they really enjoy. That's another benefit of learning to use mental images to enhance positive aspects of one's life.

Coping
with Pain

There are a few people who never feel pain. They may be afflicted by a rare genetic disorder (these people also cannot shed tears), or they may have a completely normal nervous system and brain. Either way, they usually die young. Pain is nature's warning bell, alerting us that something has gone wrong in our bodies.

For most of us, however, a completely painless existence may seem like an ideal situation. Many of us fear pain more than we fear death. But would you really not want to know until gangrene sets in that an arm or a leg has been fractured? Or never feel a twinge until it becomes evident that your appendix has ruptured? Or notice only after blisters and redness appear (or when someone else warns you) that you are sitting on a red-hot radiator? The chances are that you will accept pain if you realize that it's an early warning system, telling you to not just stand or sit there, but to *do* something to remedy the painful situation.

But once you've been warned, you usually want to get rid of the pain, particularly if it's severe or chronic. And you may find that often there is not much a doctor can do for you except to tell you to take two aspirin, go to bed, and call tomorrow if things don't improve. The whole question of the basic nature of pain is so baffling and complex that, until quite recently, most medical schools did not deal with the subject per se. Doctors were taught how to treat disease; few knew much about how to deal with patients in severe and chronic pain, except to give them mild analgesics (like aspirin) which are valuable up to a certain point, or to prescribe strong narcotics (like morphine) which work on severe pain but are unfortunately highly addictive. In cases of extreme suffering, surgeons sometimes cut nerve paths to end the transmission of pain symptoms to the brain.

As Americans live longer, the kinds of diseases that cause chronic pain—arthritis, rheumatism, and cancer, for instance—become more common. In recent years, therefore, interest in pain control among medical professionals has increased. We now see university-affiliated pain clinics that work with patients specifically to help them control pain associated with chronic illness. There is a new medical specialty called *dorology,* the science of pain. Physicians, physiologists, chemists, and biologists are working together to analyze the subtle mix of emotion and physiology that is part of the sensation we call pain.

Because emotions play a very strong part in pain and suffering, psychologists and psychiatrists have also become interested in the subject. Observers have known for a long time that some people seem to have a much higher threshold of pain than others. In objective laboratory tests, scientists have found that a mild electric shock that makes one person scream may cause another merely to wince uncomfortably and yet a third to continue talking pleasantly without seeming to feel anything at all.

Being somewhat impervious to pain is often considered a virtue by those who work with sick people. Nurses on a hospital floor tend to divide **91** their patients into two categories: the good ones who don't complain, often because they have a relatively low pain threshold; and "crocks" who tend to complain a lot. The so-called good patients tend to get more attention than the "crocks," and this treatment leads to a vicious circle. The already uncomfortable patients often wait longer to have their bells answered than the patients who do not seek help and comfort because they simply have not felt the pain. So patients who let everyone know that they are feeling "just fine, thank you" tend to make psychological gains; they are praised for their bravery and virtue. However, the patients who admit to feeling miserable and ask for relief are at a psychological disadvantage; since they make those who care for them uncomfortable, they may find that they get exhortation—"It can't be as bad as all that"—instead of sympathy or relief.

Nobody can describe pain accurately. It's a series of complex sensations that can prick, ache, or burn. It may be a steady throbbing or a series of sharp jabs or cramps. A generation ago, neurologists tried to label the kinds of pain their patients were suffering. This turned out to be an inadequate method. Today, medical science tends to define pain as a sensation that is painful. This is not very illuminating, but it's not as limiting as the old definition either.

Nor is anyone really sure exactly what causes pain. Scientists in the nineteenth century used the newly invented telephone as an analogy: pain nerves, like telephone wires, connect to a mental switchboard, they said. When the nerves are stimulated, signals are sent to the brain that are felt as pain. Today's scientists feel that this theory leaves out an important component in the stimulus-response syndrome: it ignores the role of emotion.

Physiologists and psychologists have noted that a person who is totally involved in an activity or experience may not even notice pain. A long-distance runner or swimmer will stretch his or her nerve reserves to the utmost, but won't collapse until the end of the race. Firefighters and police officers have been known to continue on duty in spite of severe and painful injuries, seemingly without being aware of their problems until the emergency passed. Only then would they become aware of the fact that they had been badly hurt, often to the point of needing massive doses of narcotics to suppress their agony.

In the days before anesthesia, alcohol was used as a pain-killer. We have all seen Western movies in which the hero takes a quick drink from a whiskey bottle before Old Doc goes to work on his injured leg with a pocket knife. The popular notion that alcoholics drown their pain in their favorite beverage does seem to have several grains of scientific truth. However, recent research seems to prove that alcohol works as a pain suppressant *only if the patient thinks it will and has used it before with good results.* If one took into consideration only the chemical properties of the drug alcohol, the non-habitual drinker should feel a stronger analgesic or anesthetic effect than the alcoholic. Researchers maintain that the belief that alcohol will combat pain is as important as the chemical action that alcohol has on the brain.

Scientists have also noted that when we expect relief from pain, we are apt to feel better. There have been controlled studies in which one group of patients has been given placebos (an inactive substance that resembles a medication but that has no effect) and another group has been given analgesics with proven effectiveness. Often it turned out that the patients given the placebos received about the same relief as those getting the real medicine. Advertisements for over-the-counter pain medicines operate on a similar principle. The principal effective ingredient in almost all of these remedies is aspirin. Some contain a few additional ingredients of somewhat dubious medical effectiveness. But consumers, believing that the combination drugs are indeed stronger, continue to buy them because the sufferers really feel more pain relief. It's their minds or their emotions that add to the effectiveness of the medication, not that mysterious ingredient that is hawked in the ads. But don't dismiss the placebo effect just because "it's in the mind." We need to understand the *mechanism* by which our thoughts and expectations actually do influence our experiences of pain or other bodily reactions. Images of relief and recovery may be playing a very important role in actually changing our emotions or our physiological responses.

Recently, many over-the-counter drugs have been appearing in capsule rather than in pill form. Capsules cost more to produce than pills, so they are more expensive for the consumer: 100 units of one analgesic capsule cost $6.95, a bottle of 100 aspirin in the same store was $.98; and both had approximately the same amount of a pain-relieving drug. Asked why manufacturers were bothering to manufacture the more expensive capsules, one marketing researcher pointed out that customers were buying them because they *expected* more relief from a red and blue capsule than from a plain white pill. "Patients are accustomed to taking prescription pain-killers that are manufactured in capsule form," this expert said. "The nonprescription medicine has, up till now, usually been a plain white pill. The consumer translates the feeling of relief he got from a doctor-prescribed capsule into what he expects from an over-the-counter capsule. So...we find that there's a very real market for an analgesic that costs 600 percent more when it's put up in a fancy format."

Physicians dealing with certain medical specialties in which pain is an almost inevitable by-product have found that a patient who can be sufficiently distracted by exercises or activities that stimulate the mind may feel no pain at all, or at least find pain bearable without drugs. The most obvious example is childbirth. So-called "natural" childbirth (meaning labor and birth with no drugs) is based on a system of breathing, exercise, and concentration that is practiced long before the birth occurs and that certainly serves to distract the woman from the discomfort she would feel. Both the Read and Lamaze methods employ these exercises, and both require a period of practice before the expected birth of a child. The breathing techniques used by the two systems are entirely different, but, for some women, either or both seem to work. Many obstetricians and midwives feel that a difficult crossword puzzle, yoga, or any other activity requiring intense concentration would work as well.

Dentists have also noticed that patients who are distracted from what's happening to their teeth often need considerably less Novocain. Some dentists have installed hi-fi equipment in their offices which plays soothing music. In addition to keeping the patient's mind occupied, the music also tends to mask the sound of the dental drill, which seems to bother some patients more than the actual drilling procedure. In some cases the patient holds onto a switch with which he or she can adjust the volume on the radio or tape machine depending on the need for distraction from the pain or the fear of it.

Scientists who have done research in pain sometimes ask that the patient, as part of the experimental process, record exactly how much discomfort is being experienced at a given moment. They have noticed that there is rarely a consistently high or low level of pain all the time. The disagreeable sensations tend to fluctuate. Sometimes the very effort itself that the subject makes in recording responses seems to lessen the awareness of pain.

The next step in this kind of research is to find methods that will help patients use their own resources of mind and emotion to cope with pain. At the University of Waterloo in Canada, a group of researchers has done just that. Drs. Donald Meichenbaum and Dennis Turk have set up a whole series of experiments and devised approaches to teach people how to deal with pain. They ask their subjects to immerse their hands in freezing cold water until the painful sensations become too uncomfortable to withstand. They are allowed to remove their hands whenever they wish. The researchers have found that some people cannot stand the cold longer than a minute whereas others are quite able to maintain control for up to five minutes. (Nine minutes is the outside limit of endurance; after that frostbite or freezing becomes a factor, and of course no research subject is allowed to take such a risk.)

The two doctors found that people who can withstand the physical discomfort longest are those who engage in a variety of mental activities while their hands are in the water. These people know how to relax sufficiently to allow their minds to wander to more pleasant subjects. They may picture themselves in a warm, sunny climate, or sitting in front of a blazing fire in a ski lodge, or immersed in a nice, warm bath.

Some will imagine themselves to be heroic characters of fact or fiction, the kind of people who can withstand pain without flinching; a football or ice hockey star, a brave knight, or a bionic man or woman may do very well. Others picture themselves in some very exciting activity: they are driving a car along a beautiful but dangerous mountain pass, they are schussing down a snow-covered mountain, they are playing a championship tennis game with Billie Jean King.

More intellectual types may keep themselves busy by working out a complicated mathematical equation or trying to remember a Shakespearean sonnet. As long as the imagined activity or exercise is absorbing enough, it will probably serve as a pain control.

Meichenbaum and Turk also noted that those research subjects who have a set of coping strategies which they learned in advance of the painful situation usually do much better than those who at-

96

tempt this technique for the first time after the pain has started. Of course, the hospitals and clinics that make "prepared childbirth" classes available to pregnant women know these facts, and women who had taken such classes were at an advantage in these experiments.

An important factor in pain control through mind exercises is the patient's attitude toward the experience and his or her sense of confidence in the effectiveness of the technique. A person in pain who can say: "I can cope...that first surge really was bad but this one is not so bad that I can't stand it," will do better than one who thinks: "I'm a brave and wonderful person and therefore I will grit my teeth and bear it all!" The specific images or set of coping thoughts are more effective than just a verbal cliché.

Since all of us can expect to have to bear pain at some time in our lives, it's a good idea to learn coping techniques long before they are needed. We don't require the pain stimulus to do the appropriate exercises. We can use the techniques just to pass the time of day: they are usually pleasant and fun.

This is how the exercise session should proceed:

1. Do the relaxation exercises described in Chapter 5.

2. When you are completely relaxed, imagine that you are in a dentist's office or some other situation in which you may expect to experience pain.

3. You will find that your muscles tense up. Do the relaxation exercises again.

4. Practice these exercises until you can relax at will. At that point, switch to a beautiful and/or comfortable scene: place yourself at a beach, a ski lodge, etc. Stay there for a while. Keeping your eyes closed will prevent you from becoming distracted.

5. Open your eyes, get up, and stretch; you are now no longer in the relaxed state or in your imaginary hideaway.

6. Do the relaxation exercises again, and this time picture yourself in an exciting, stimulating activity: driving a car, skiing, playing tennis, etc. Keep this scene going for a while, then open your eyes and get up, and you are out of your imaginary world again.

7. Do the relaxation exercises again. This time try being your favorite hero or heroine. This is your chance to be anyone you want to be: a famous athlete, a symphony orchestra conductor, a physician performing the world's most outstanding surgery, or an attorney winning complicated cases for widows and orphans against impossible odds. Put yourself through a whole series of activities as your imaginary character. After a while, get up, stretch, and the exercise is over.

The reason for trying out several different imaginary places, situations, and people is to find out for yourself what works best for you. You may enjoy every one of the exercises and not be able to decide if you want to use one or all until you have actually used them in a painful situation. The next time you visit the dentist or have a bad headache, try a variety of approaches. You may find that you do better by remaining with just one kind of mind picture than by using several in succession.

Even if you can make this system work for you, and most people can, you will, of course, not be able to avoid all pain. There will be times when you will still need two aspirin, a hot water bottle, a Novocain injection, or even a shot of morphine or Demerol. But you will find there are dozens of situations in which you can get at least some relief with the imagery-based pain-coping techniques; consequently, you may need less medicine than if you are concentrating on how miserable you feel.

How to Improve
Bad Moods
and Overcome Insomnia

All of us occasionally have bad days and nights—days in which everything seems to conspire to make us feel blue and miserable, and nights in which we toss and turn trying to solve all the problems left over from the rotten day. Usually we tell ourselves that we can't help the way we feel, that there's nothing much we can do except to wait for our emotional landscape to brighten. Or, all too frequently, we take a mood-changing drug. But there are ways we can help to make ourselves feel better and to relax sufficiently without chemicals of any kind—to be able to drop off to sleep and then tackle all those unsolved difficulties energetically the next morning.

BAD MOODS We know, of course, that we can sometimes cope with negative emotions, such as anger, hostility, fear, anxiety, and jealousy, by talking them out. After all, an important principle of psychotherapy is based on this assumption. But often there's nobody to whom we want to talk. If we have only ourselves to work with, we can use our fantasies and imaginations to help us overcome the inevitable bad times. In that way, we may be able to substitute positive emotions for negative ones. This is a good skill to acquire, not just because it will get us through some difficult times, but also because a constant stream of negative emotions, combined with insomnia, can produce the kind of stress on our bodies that may cause real physical difficulties. Prolonged worry, tension, and desperation can hasten the emergence of the stress-related diseases, such as ulcers, high' blood pressure, and migraine headaches, perhaps even certain forms of cancer.

Over the years, there have been many books and pseudo-psychological theories that have said almost exactly that, usually in several hundred pages of closely set type. Coué's theory, "Day by day in every way, I'm getting better and better," was fashionable in the early part of this century. During the 1950's the power of positive thinking was supposed to make us healthy, wealthy, and wise. And remember that great swing number of the 1940's "Accentuate the Positive!"

The difference between "positive thinking" or Couéism and current psychological methods of changing moods is worth mentioning. Taking an upbeat orientation, a constructive view, is always useful for getting one through difficult periods and keeping oneself going. Philosophers or deeply thoughtful scientists like Schopenhauer, Nietzsche, Russell, and Freud were able to recognize the tragedies inherent in human existence and the evil that does pervade our world, yet they persisted in their efforts to clarify our understanding through their writings. In a sense, despite their pessimism about human perfectibility they continued to strive to help people see life more clearly. Thus, despite much inner despair, they took a constructive view of their own work and expressed themselves in the act of writing or teaching.

The problem for most people is that slogans like "Keep your chin up" soon seem empty. The recent developments in psychology and psycho-physiology suggest that if we can recognize the specific *mechanisms* of the body and mind that are closely tied to negative, self-defeating moods, we can begin to provide specific strategies for modifying them. Recent research on the role of the face in human emotions, pioneered by Professor Silvan Tomkins at Princeton University and developed further experimentally by Carroll Izard at the University of Delaware, Paul Ekman at the Langley-Porter Clinic in San Francisco, and Gary Schwartz at both Harvard and Yale, have demonstrated that phrases like "Downcast," "Keep your chin up," or "Keep a stiff upper lip" really do reflect very basic emotional and motivational reactions. And recent work by Schwartz and various other investigators has suggested that actually changing our facial expressions from sadness to the muscular reactions of a smile can influence our moods.

We are still learning about the musculature and psychophysiology of our emotions. But there is increasing evidence that the use of specific, goal-directed images can produce important and useful changes in our feelings and help us to get on with more constructive actions.

We can't promise help for every depressed or bitter person with the techniques we will mention; but unlike some of our predecessors, we do have some scientific basis for proposing that they're worth a try.

In experiments at Yale University and at the West Haven VA Hospital in Connecticut, a psychologist, Dr. David Schultz, got some remarkable results with severely depressed patients in a number of veterans' hospitals by encouraging them to develop elaborate, cheerful fantasies. They were urged to imagine that they had won a lottery, or were about to enjoy a special meal at the best restaurant in town, or that someone whom they especially admired had complimented them. Another group of veterans who were hostile as well as depressed were encouraged to engage in fantasies in which they retaliated against the people who had hurt them. Still another group was asked to fantasize about beautiful nature scenes. All three groups became less depressed as they were able to create more imaginative mind images. Members of a control group, who were not given this opportunity for directed imagery but who were encouraged simply to allow their images to develop naturally, continued in their cycle of depression. Especially good results were obtained with the fantasies that depicted increased self-esteem or that satisfied the need for affection and approval, and also with the purely peaceful nature type of fantasies. Fantasies of aggression are probably not nearly as useful.

To begin with, no matter how complicated the problem is, or how remote the solution seems, it's always a good idea to try to relax. The idea that working under tension will produce better results than working while calm and secure probably originated with military officers. Relaxed soldiers, generally speaking, don't feel much like fighting. The concept may then have been adopted by Little League baseball coaches and major league ice hockey team owners who wanted their players straining at the bit. From there, the idea probably gravitated to various types of bosses who somehow got the impression that setting impossible deadlines, sales quotas, and so on would improve their employees' performances. Not so. In general, tense people do sloppy work, and insomniacs tend to doze off at their desks or drink enough coffee to make them jittery.

So, the first step to take when faced with a problem that causes a bad mood is to relax, using the relaxation exercises in Chapter 5. The next step is to dissolve all that unhappiness in a little humor. Remembering funny scenes from your life, from television programs, or from the movies can help immeasurably in lightening a bad day or a miserable night. Let's tackle the bad days first. (The second part of this chapter will deal with insomnia.)

Remember our old friend Eleanor Beatty, the temporarily retired art teacher who is presently a harassed mother and homemaker? She uses a combination of humor and the ability to paint bright and attractive scenes in her mind, instead of on a canvas, to lighten her mood on days when two of the children have the flu, there are three loads of laundry to be done, and her husband is bringing home a colleague for dinner. The fact that she is an artist helps, of course. But even if we can't color a child's paint book or draw a straight line in real life we all can paint Rembrandts or Miros in our fantasies. Eleanor drew funny cartoons in her mind. She could always entertain herself, during brief moments of relaxation in her frantic day, by putting her fantasies to work. That is the basic difference between her and Joan Anders, for instance. Joan sinks into a depression at the very thought of a dull day, then she gravitates toward the refrigerator for a fattening snack. John Powers heads for the liquor cabinet to pour himself a fast Scotch. So, while Eleanor is reasonably slim, happy, and sober, Joan is overweight and miserable, and John is frustrated and drunk.

Eleanor Beatty discovered for herself the same benefit of directed imagination that emerged from Dr. Schultz's research on chronically depressed patients. She learned on her own that images that are organized specifically to increase self-esteem, or to distract the mind from the things one can't do anything about by shifting one's thoughts to beautiful nature scenes, may be particularly effective in changing moods. If images of peaceful nature scenes or fantasies about being praised or fed or loved can make a difference for those hospitalized veterans, it would seem that they would also be effective under less drastic circumstances. Dr. Schultz has also tried some of these methods with normal individuals and obtained good results.

104 Research and clinical work with normal individuals

who complained of feeling depressed or bored and restless has also supported the value of such specific imagery in changing moods and in providing a basis for coping with the underlying problems more effectively.

One of the problems of being in a foul mood is that it has a snowballing effect. We often find ourselves going from bad to worse, criticizing others suddenly and sharply so that they react in anger at us, and this only makes our mood even darker. The critical thing, therefore, is that while these self-esteem or nature fantasies may not resolve the basic underlying difficulties of an individual, they can, at least temporarily, break the cyclic effect of an unpleasant mood and lead one to confront the situation with a clearer head and a better chance to make an appropriate decision.

The *New England Journal of Medicine,* a highly respected medical publication for physicians, published in its December 1976 issue an article by Norman Cousins, editor of *Saturday Review.* Mr. Cousins had become seriously ill after a long and exhausting business trip to Russia. His symptoms were alarming as well as miserable. He suffered from excruciating arthritis-like pains in his joints and in his back. He was hospitalized for weeks, almost unable to move, and was given vast amounts of pain-killing drugs with no sign of improvement. His doctor told him that he was not sure that a normal life would ever again become possible.

Mr. Cousins decided to fight back—with laughter instead of drugs. It turned out later that he had actually been allergic to one of the medications he had been taking; it was producing hives all over his body which, he said, made his skin feel as if it "was being chewed up by millions of red ants." At any rate, he set out systematically to teach himself to laugh again, a skill that he had almost forgotten during those painful months in bed. He did not decide to do this on a sudden impulse either. He had carefully studied medical journals, books,

105

and other materials that detailed the physical effects of stress on the body. He came to the conclusion that if negative emotion could have negative chemical effects on physical health, then positive emotions might perhaps have positive effects. "Is it possible that love, hope, faith, laughter, confidence, and the will to live have therapeutic value?" he asked. "Do chemical changes occur only on the down side?"

Obviously, putting the positive emotions to work is not as simple as turning on a garden hose, he decided. But he would try to work systematically to control his emotions. First, he decided to replace anxiety with a "fair degree of confidence." He discussed his plan with his doctor, who apparently thought that what Mr. Cousins had in mind certainly would not hurt. It might even help, since nothing else had so far. Mr. Cousins started his regime at the hospital. Taking no drugs but Vitamin C, he began a program which called for the full exercise of affirmative emotions as a factor in enhancing body chemistry. "It was easy enough to hope and love and have faith," he wrote, "but what about laughter? Nothing is less funny than being flat on your back with all the bones in your spine and joints hurting." He decided to start with a series of amusing television movies. Because of his profession as an editor and journalist, he was luckier than most of us. He had access to a motion picture projector and some old, funny television films. A nurse helped him to run the projector, and the experiment was off to a good start.

"It worked," Mr. Cousins said. "I made the joyous discovery that ten minutes of genuine belly laughter had an anesthetic effect and would give me at least two hours of painless sleep. When the pain-killing of the laughter wore off, we would switch on the motion picture projector again, and, not infrequently, it would lead to another pain-free sleep interval." When he got tired of movies, his nurse was asked to read really funny books to him.

The only negative side effect of this experiment was that some of the patients in neighboring rooms complained about all the laughter. So, Mr. Cousins decided to move his show out of the hospital and into a hotel. He continued his therapy program there, and, within eight days he improved sufficiently to be able to move his thumbs without pain. Two weeks later he and his wife went to an island resort, and within a few days he was standing by himself. His recovery continued, and in 1976 the ex-patient reported that he was playing tennis, riding a horse (while taking pictures at the same time), and playing Bach's *Toccata and Fugue in D Minor* on the organ. Perhaps even more important for all those who admire that fine magazine, the *Saturday Review*, he is back at work.

He credits his laugh therapy, combined with huge doses of Vitamin C, for his recovery. Since we are not physicians, we cannot comment on the merits of the vitamin therapy. But this carefully documented example, according to the patient's own records, would seem to show that negative emotions, anxiety, and anger in particular, increase physical pain. Relaxation and serenity, on the other hand, can make that pain a lot more bearable.

Nor would we need the motion picture projector and films which Mr. Cousins used to make his trips easier and more graphic. We can probably accomplish a good deal without such an elaborate arrangement, particularly when we are dealing with day-to-day fluctuations of mood, or even mild, persistent feelings of depression or anxiety. We can recreate in our heads those funny scenes we enjoyed in our favorite movie or TV shows and replay them again and again, almost as vividly as if we had an actual projector on hand. What's more, we can carry some of these scenes even further than the actors and writers that created them. We are not limited by what's on tape or film; we have our fantasies to take all those funny moments to whatever limits we care to set for ourselves.

107

How would you begin to accomplish this if you've never tried before? You might want to start with a specific book or movie that you particularly enjoyed. Try to remember, as graphically as possible, the scenes that made you laugh the most. One co-author of this book is especially fond of Woody Allen movies and reruns scenes from those over and over in his head. When Woody comes up with a new movie, additional scenes from it are added to the already large inventory of possibilities in the author's head.

He likes one scene from *Take the Money and Run,* in which Woody attempts to hold up a bank by passing a note to the teller to turn over all the available cash. The trouble is that Woody's handwriting is so rotten that the teller can't make out the request. First he calls another teller, then the manager, and finally a vice-president to try to decipher what his weird customer has in mind. While the group confers, Woody gets more and more nervous—and finally decamps with a failed holdup on his hands.

Lately, scenes from *Annie Hall* have been added to the daydream scenario. There are all those times when Woody, in his head, imagines that he stops unlikely looking persons on a New York street to ask them intimate questions about their lives so that he can compare notes with his own. It is, of course, entirely possible to take Woody out of that picture altogether and to imagine *yourself* doing something like this.

The other author of this book replays scenes from the *Mary Tyler Moore Show* and *Mary Hartman, Mary Hartman* in her head. She regrets that both TV programs are off the air now, but feels that they will provide her with a few good laughs for many years to come. She also recalls old Art Buchwald columns, and occasionally invents a new tag line which she is convinced is even funnier than what Buchwald wrote.

108   A sense of humor is almost as personal as a

thumbprint. So whatever provokes you to laugh will probably work for you.

Another trick is to remember scenes from your past that seem especially funny. Sometimes these scenes may be funny only to you because of the setting in which they took place or the particular individual involved. Again, one of the co-authors remembers a time, many years ago, when he and his wife took their young son to Macy's Thanksgiving Day Parade. The 5-year-old boy had bought himself a fake cigarette at a novelty store and was puffing "smoke" when a woman stopped him, bent over, and asked, "Little boy, aren't you too young to smoke?" He just looked up at her and said, "Lady, I'm a midget."

As one replays a scene like that in one's mind, one usually starts to remember other pleasant incidents with the same person, or other amusing scenes with different characters. Enough of this kind of imagery can begin to make quite a difference even during the gloomiest of moods.

Then there are those days in which everything seems to go wrong all at once. Household appliances break down and repairmen fail to show up. Department stores deliver the wrong merchandise, a septic tank overflows, or you get a notice from the bank that your checking account is overdrawn. Naturally, the best remedy for dealing with the bad mood growing out of such events is to take effective action to correct them, but often there are periods of time when you are literally powerless to change the situation.

One way to modify this pattern is to use fantasies, at least temporarily, as an escape from the situation. Here again the fantasy can be mixed with a certain amount of wild humor. Just imagine leaving that nest in the suburbs and taking a job as a butler or maid in a super-rich household, with summers on a yacht and winters in a chalet in Aspen or at a beach house on the Riviera. Or how about winning a trip around the world in one of **109** those lotteries that various magazines distribute to increase their circulation? After all, you did mail in your entry blank six months ago, didn't you? What about imagining a call from the White House announcing that Jimmy Carter is about to drop in on *you*?...But first, of course, the Army Corps of Engineers will have to fix the septic tank and the broken television set. Or just imagine that the bank manager personally calls you to let you know that he is *terribly* embarrassed about the fact that the bank mixed up *your* name with that of one of your disreputable neighbors. You might even try all of the fantasies simultaneously, or in sequence. Fantasies of this kind are not going to correct the underlying problems or the plumbing, but they may well prevent you from getting deeper and deeper into the quagmire of a gray depression.

Sometimes it is useful, just as an exercise, to deliberately develop a backlog of mind trips from material you have read in books or seen in the movies or from personal memories on which you can call in times of stress. It's a good idea to write some of these down. Think about the possibility of keeping a regular journal of some of the really funny scenes you see in movies, read in books, or enjoy on television. Of course, writing things down never quite captures all the richness of the scene, but that's where your own vivid memory and basic imagery capacity can help considerably. Writing down the material is simply a quick way to make sure that you can retrieve the material from your memory easily. Once you start on the image, your mind can elaborate on it. The more vividly you can visualize the scene, the more fully can you express the accompanying emotion.

We all know the pleasure we can get from looking at old photographs or watching movies of ourselves or our children. The interesting thing is that your brain has the capacity to generate an even greater variety of material once you have stimulated it through some of the memories we have suggested. What you need to do is to take these memories a step further. Imagine the situation in its most absurd possibilities. For instance, imagine the dignified high school principal whom you never liked very much (perhaps he reminds you of Mr. Woodman in *Welcome Back, Kotter*) losing his pants on the podium while he gives the graduation address.

Incidentally, don't take all our suggestions literally. Use your own resources. You have within you similar capacities for thinking up the hilarious situations that Woody Allen or Art Buchwald have used professionally, and flipping them around at will.

Sometimes, just by changing your bleak mood, you may be able to take more effective action to help solve the real-life problems that are getting you down.

Obviously, in and of themselves, imagery and fantasy used to reduce negative emotions won't solve your actual problems. You can't fix the TV set or the septic tank by fantasy, nor can you pay your overdue income tax with mind movies. But what a happy fantasy *can* do for you is to break you out of that self-defeating mind set that may lead you to do irrational or impulsive things, like writing a letter of resignation you don't really mean, or shouting at your children, or having a few drinks too many. Or your bleak mood may leave you feeling so helpless that you can't take any remedial action at all. So, by changing those unpleasant negative emotions through fantasy and humor, you may be able to act more effectively in the real world. In this sense the most extreme escapist fantasies need not be seen as withdrawal from real life, but rather as genuine methods to increase your effectiveness in dealing with the practical problems that confront you.

According to one recent survey, more than half of all Americans over 15 years of age have occasional problems with sleeplessness. More strikingly yet,

INSOMNIA

about 15 percent indicate that they have chronic difficulties falling asleep and/or staying asleep, and another third of the population has recurrent bouts of insomnia.

Not surprisingly, then, there is a large and growing market for sleeping pills. In 1975, the last year for which the figures were available, more than 5 million prescriptions for Seconal were filled by druggists throughout the country. Seconal is just one of 30 or so barbiturate combinations, and we can assume that the total number of barbiturate prescriptions probably topped 10 million each year. There is no question that a hefty dose of a barbiturate will put you to sleep. The problem with these drugs is, however, that they are physically addictive. Anyone who has taken barbiturate preparations over a long period of time knows that, in order for them to remain effective, the dose has to be increased steadily. A genuine case of barbiturate addiction is a serious matter; physicians often find that withdrawal from these drugs is more difficult and more dangerous than withdrawal from heroin.

There are also dozens of prescription pills with a different chemistry, strong doses of tranquilizers, for instance. These medications are not as potentially damaging as barbiturates, but they too have some built-in problems. Tranquilizers are apparently not physically addictive, but they may be psychologically habit-forming.

Then there are all those nonprescription sleep preparations with which people dose themselves in order to escape from those long, miserable, wakeful nights. The trouble with over-the-counter pills and capsules is that they are probably ineffective and therefore a waste of money (the FDA is at present looking into this possibility with the intention of forcing some of the worst offenders off the market).

It is clear from all of this that our society has become too dependent upon barbiturates, tranquilizers, and over-the-counter preparations which, while they may sometimes work, also generate additional problems and side effects.

Researchers in sleep laboratories have noted that those drugs which are the most effective are also those which interfere with the deepest and most relaxing kind of sleep: the so-called Stage 1 EEG, rapid-eye-movement sleep (REM). All barbiturates, for instance, produce abnormal sleep in which the rapid eye movements, often associated with vivid dreamlike sleep, are suppressed. Tranquilizers may also have this effect. What's more, many prescription sleep medicines have not left the body when you awaken in the morning. A single dose of barbital will show traces in the urine eight to twelve *days* after a single dose. Phenobarbital (the principal ingredient of Seconal and Nembutal) is eliminated very slowly from the body over a period of several days. No wonder you feel groggy in the morning after taking one of these drugs. Of course, there are times when most of us need artificial aid to sleep: the night before an operation in a hospital, for instance. But for that run-of-the-mill tossing and turning that seems to happen to all of us, drugs probably do more harm than good, and all the while the help we need is available from our imagination and fantasy.

What are the most frequent causes of what we might call "healthy insomnia" as opposed to the kind of sleeplessness that we experience when we are truly sick? It is usually caused by the unfinished activities of the day that we keep recirculating in our heads at night. If we did not finish writing a particular report, balancing a set of books, bringing the car in for a checkup, or if we have not finished working on our income tax return, there is very little we can do about it at three o'clock in the morning. But what's keeping us awake is still firmly lodged in our minds. The best method to unlodge it is to concentrate on something else, preferably something that's interesting enough to keep us going, and relaxing enough to allow us to go to

113

sleep. The critical feature, then, for dealing with the various types of unfinished business that recur in our heads is to shift attention away from them to something more mildly interesting but still not *so* interesting that it, in itself, will keep us awake.

Whoever thought first of counting sheep as a method of sleep therapy had the kernel of a good idea. But unless you are a sheep farmer in the Australian bush, mentally watching all those sheep hopping over a fence can get pretty dreary. It isn't likely to be interesting enough to keep your attention away from those recurring thoughts about the unfinished report at the office or the dirty laundry in the cellar. Most of us tend to feel that when you've seen one sheep, you've seen them all. So, a better course is to find an interesting scene of your own, preferably one that requires some kind of mental manipulation and that is sufficiently absorbing to take front stage, away from the leftover worries of the day.

In interviewing a large number of people about how they cope with problems of sleeplessness, we have found that many do indeed have specific techniques and sequences of images that help drive out unpleasant thoughts temporarily and allow the natural processes of sleep to take over. The techniques that people use break down into a number of categories:

1. Relieving the sense of pressure. Some people simply engage in an extended kind of relaxation exercise such as those previously discussed, or make use of meditation, in which they focus on a single word such as "one" or a "mantra" if they are involved in TM or some other exotic form of systematic meditation. Thus, even if thoughts of unfinished tasks recur, they do so with less emotional pressure behind them, and getting to sleep becomes easier.

2. Choosing a focus. Some people choose a specific problem from the recurring group that is whirling around in their heads and attempt to resolve just

this one problem in a systematic and careful way. This can work if the difficulty can be resolved just by thinking it out.

Unfortunately, an unfinished report doesn't lend itself to that approach, although one might get some good general ideas about what should be included and, therefore, feel somewhat less pressured. Certainly the undone laundry won't get clean by thinking about what kind of detergent to use or which cycle on the washing machine would be most useful.

So, one way to distract yourself from the recycling pressure is to imagine, as vividly as possible, that it *is already tomorrow,* and that you are busy coping with whatever unfinished business is still at hand. Go step-by-step through whatever processes are needed to get the task done, and imagine all the ways you will use to work the problem out. Concentrate on only one situation, not two or three, and try to keep this situation as simple as possible. In *A Diary of a Mad Housewife*, Tina Balser pictured herself as a superefficient British housekeeper, looking over her domain to make sure that everything was perfect, that is, all the closets neat, enough food and other supplies stored away for the next month, all the crockery and glasses polished and lined up on the shelves. It worked for her, and if you've read the book, you know she had more troubles than most of us.

There is an even more effective method for handling mild and sometimes moderately severe insomnia: call up a series of images that are completely unrelated to whatever problem is recycling in your head. They should be interesting, but probably not too stimulating (that might keep you awake even longer, but at least you would be pleasantly awake). One of the co-authors calls up from his memory a childhood fantasy about a favorite football or baseball team engaged in one of its many games. He loves sports, but his day-to-day activities, and therefore most of his unfinished

115

tasks, are very far removed from the locker room or the playing field. They are much more apt to concern research projects, clinical problems, or university politics. But once he has his team in place, with the first batter taking two balls and hitting a single, with the second bunting and sacrificing the runner to second base, sleep takes over quickly. The next morning he wakes up and realizes that there's a man on second with only one out. He can continue the game the next sleepless night, or start all over again with a new one. While this kind of fantasy would probably increase the problems of a worried baseball coach or sports reporter, it works surprisingly well with many sports fans whose worries lie in other directions.

The sports fan might want some variety, though. So, in the appropriate season, a football daydream may be substituted. It helps to choose a real team whose games have been interesting during the past few seasons, or even to create two teams of all-stars, to keep the fantasy from bogging down. Once a really good fantasy game gets started, it almost always runs its course automatically, and the next morning you wake to realize that the team has been left with a fourth down and two yards to go on the opponent's five-yard line.

For those of us who are not that interested in sports, there are plenty of other fantasy subjects. We know a man who imagines himself conducting a whole symphony orchestra. He pictures himself coming to the podium, tapping his baton for silence, and then letting his mind and his ears fill with the sounds of music. He prefers quieter pieces like slow movements of symphonies or serenades, and he rarely gets through more than a few bars, or half a movement at the most, before he wakes up and finds it's morning.

The other co-author has a ballet group ready and waiting in her mind. She's a writer and can't even approximate a decent Hustle on the dance floor. But in her mind she puts those ballerinas through the most intricate dances. A ballet version of Mozart's *Eine Kleine Nachtmusik* is her favorite score. Since the 1976 Olympic Games, she's added to her fantasy repertory. Skater Dorothy Hamill can be induced through imagery to perform some really fascinating dance sequences on ice. She beats those dull sheep leaping over fences any time.

For the kind of insomnia we've described, fantasy can really be effective. You have to select a daydream image that involves a sequence of steps, plays, or movements. The "story line" should be one that genuinely interests you: a game, dance, contest, or organized activity that you've already thought about a lot and that can absorb your attention. The method works remarkably well, especially if preceded by relaxation exercises such as those described in Chapter 5. What't more, it's fun and it's entirely harmless—which is more than can be said for any drug.

Empathy
and Interpersonal Skills
through Imagery
and Daydreaming

Lack of communication is blamed for all kinds of social ills, from minor marital squabbles to major international incidents. Often it is assumed that the noncommunicating participants in such unfortunate happenings are simply not talking to each other at all. But that is not always the case. Frequently they are actually spending a great deal of time talking. The problem is that whatever is being said is not being understood. The participants have their signals crossed.

We would not go so far as to suggest that the SALT talks between the United States and Russia might have been improved by using imagination and imagery, but certainly misunderstandings in marriage, in friendships, and on the job might be alleviated if either or both participants begin to develop an ability to spot the nuances of other people's behavior. The precise measurement of how we communicate a great many signals, not just with words, but with our facial expressions, body movements, and tone of voice, is a major new development in the behavior sciences.

Psychologists, sociologists, and specialists in

the new science of interpersonal communication have pointed out that we all learn to use our bodies and facial expressions to send signals to others about our intentions, conflicts, and emotions. Often we don't recognize that we are sometimes contradicting our words by our body postures. Even more seriously, we may be failing to pick up the subtle points of others' communications to us. We grow up learning to speak our native language and also to express ourselves in a local dialect or in special phrases that reflect our community or ethnic backgrounds. We also learn certain gestures that reflect our emotions or stand for particular phrases. Movies taken on the Lower East Side of New York City when Italians and Jews lived in close proximity there showed that first-generation Italians used sweeping gestures that started close to the body and moved outward. Jews used gestures that started close to the body and moved inward. The Italians used many gestures to stand for words or whole phrases; the Jews used gestures largely to emphasize or punctuate the words they were saying at the time. By the second generation these body differences began to fade as both groups became more assimilated into the American Anglo-Saxon "mainstream," but many still persist into a third generation and often can lead to some subtle differences in communication when a young man of Italian background is dating a girl from a Jewish family.

Thus while we learn a good deal about expressing or interpreting nonverbal cues within our immediate family, we may not learn enough about groups and families that are different from us. To communicate fully with others, whether in social situations, intimate relationships, or business, we have much to learn about sensing the meanings and emotions that are expressed. We are talking not only of skills or competencies that can make us effective or clever manipulators. An important, indeed a basic human capacity is to feel deeply what others are suffering or struggling with. Deep affection and love between people is expressed through mutual

121

caring and shared feelings. But many people have not learned some of the important cues that can help them sense what others are feeling; even a devoted husband or wife may not be able to recognize some of the feelings of his or her partner because of differences in upbringing or culture or because the two have not yet learned to talk more fully about private mental processes, dreams, fantasies, or the childhood fears or superstitions that we all carry into adult life.

How might these empathic skills be used in a constructive way? Let's look at a few examples:

Joan Anders, whom we met in Chapter 1, had some conflicts around her engagement to that young lawyer Alan Evans, whom all her relatives and friends considered highly suitable as a husband. One of the reasons her feminist friends approved of him was his apparent interest in her career as a TV director. But Joan has some real, if unexpressed, doubts about her fiancé. That's one of the reasons she is so anxious much of the time.

By using her imagination and fantasy, she might be able to resolve some of her doubts, or increase them enough to call off the engagement. In her mind, she can play over conversations she has had with Alan recently. There was that time she told him about a special news show she was planning. He seemed to listen, but he looked half asleep. At the end of her enthusiastic description of all the people who would have to be interviewed for the show, he said: "That's really very interesting, dear," and then launched into a monologue about the kind of furniture he would like to see in their future home. Another time she was very worried about getting a promotion. Alan seemed to be listening sympathetically, but then he dropped a remark: "Well, it really won't matter so much once we are married....I make enough money for both of us. So why don't you relax?" In playing over these dialogues in her mind, Joan might well be able to put her finger on what's bothering her about her prospective husband. He seems to repeat all the right feminist clichés and use all the proper Women's Movement terms, but is he perhaps in his heart of hearts a typical male chauvinist after all? Perhaps he hasn't fully recognized that what he really wants is to have her exchange her place behind the TV camera for a place in front of the kitchen stove once the wedding is over. Obviously, Joan will have to get some answers to these questions *before* she gets married, or her marriage might end in disaster fairly early on.

John Powers heads for the liquor cabinet after his regular 4 P.M. meeting with his boss. If anyone took his blood pressure at that time, they'd probably notice a decided rise. Why? His boss has not said anything antagonistic, threatening, or even critical. He hardly ever does. But then, he rarely says anything complimentary either. If John replays those conversations in his head, he may discover that he wants more warmth and appreciation than he is receiving from the boss. The man's coolness really bothers him. John finds himself daydreaming about going to work for another man he knows in the same industry. Actually, he realizes that his present job is a better one than the other fellow can offer. But as he thinks about the fantasy, he realizes that the other boss has a warmth, a willingness to offer praise or personal attention that his present supervisor lacks.

After John discovers why he becomes upset after these meetings, he can decide whether he has good reason for feeling so insecure, that is, whether the lack of praise and warmth indicates that there's a problem between him and the boss, or whether he is just expecting an unreasonable amount of praise from a man who is just not a warm, outgoing person. Once he has discovered for himself, by using his intuition and imagination, what's behind his anxiety about those meetings, he may be able to take more appropriate action than pouring himself an extra slug of Scotch.

123

Here are a few steps you may want to take in order to understand better what another person is trying to convey:

Learn to listen to meanings behind words, as well as to words themselves.

Take a simple sentence: "Thank you very much for your courtesy." What does it mean? Well, that depends on how it is said. It can mean just what is seems to mean: Someone is grateful to you for being so nice. Or it can be as formal as the closing on a business letter. Or it can be tinged with sarcasm. For instance, picture this scene: A passenger is getting out of a New York taxicab and hands the driver a ten-cent tip.

Passenger: "That's all I have on me in change."
Driver: "Thank you very much for your courtesy."

Or it can be a simple sentence laced with a good deal of bitterness:

Wife (picking up her suitcase prior to making an exit on her way to Reno): "I thought it would be only right to let you know that, on the advice of my lawyer, I took all the stocks out of the safe deposit box this morning. I just thought you should know..."
Husband: "Thank you very much for your courtesy."

In these situations, it would be obvious that there is more to that seemingly formal phrase than appears on the surface. But in other situations this might not be as obvious, so careful listening for nuances is necessary.

Start looking carefully at facial expressions.
Often you will be able to understand what another person is trying to communicate, even if

he or she is speaking a foreign language, simply by watching the person's expressions.

There is an increasingly large body of psychological literature in the area of communication through facial expression. Psychologists Silvan Tomkins, Paul Ekman, and Carroll Izard have noted several distinct facial expressions, each reflecting a different emotion—fear, anger, surprise, sadness, interest, and joy—that human beings share all over the world. In some important experiments, Ekman showed that natives of New Guinea who could neither read nor write, and who had scarcely been exposed to Western civilization, could clearly identify a basic group of emotions from the expressions on the faces of Europeans and Americans. Americans could do the same with the photographs of New Guineans who expressed emotions of disgust, happiness, sadness, and anger.

Actually, this kind of experience with interpersonal communication starts very early in life. Psychologist Michael Ellis has described how mothers and babies interact. The babies do not understand the meaning of words but they do understand the mothers' smiles. Almost all babies, after about the age of three months, will try to imitate the way the mother looks and sounds. So when the mother smiles, the baby smiles back. When she says: "goo goo" or "ga ga" the baby will try to imitate the sounds. Actually, that's the way they learn to speak. And the mother reacts to the baby's attempted imitation by repeating the situation again. Through this repetitive play, the baby begins to experience a sense of self-efficacy; the child seems to be acquiring the knowledge that he or she can influence the environment, in this case, the mother. Out of this mutual interaction, trust develops between mothers and babies, not just as play but as a very basic experience for the child.

Apparently, children pay this kind of close attention to expressions and nuances almost automatically. But as adults, we have to some extent **125** lost our ability to understand what is not obvious on the surface. We listen to the sounds of speech, but we don't look at the speaker.

Realize that in some cultures and for some individuals, control of emotion, and therefore of facial expression, has become a socially accepted necessity.

We talk of the British stiff upper lip, for instance. For some groups of English men and women this is not just a figure of speech, it's a fact of life. Nor is this true just of the population of the British Isles. In the United States we apparently still expect our leaders to show a minimum of emotion. According to popular legend, Senator Muskie of Maine lost the 1972 Democratic nomination for the presidency when he broke into tears on a snowy New Hampshire campaign trip. No one was really sure he cried (that moisture might have been melting snowflakes) and even if he did, he had a good reason: a local newspaper had published a particularly nasty story maligning his wife. But still, a lot of Americans felt suspicious of a man who could break into tears under stress.

The two 1976 presidential candidates were actually allowed a few tears: Ford when he returned to his hometown in Michigan the afternoon before election day, and Carter just after he had been elected; he was facing a group of friends and standing next to his mother in his hometown of Plains, Georgia. But some mothers, all over the country, probably still tell their little sons, "Boys don't cry." So, when you are faced with an apparently emotionless individual, it's important to understand that very few people feel nothing; some are just better at hiding their feelings than others. When you are dealing with such a person, it becomes even more important to use your intuitive powers and your imagination to understand their message correctly.

When dealing with people whom you wish to

understand, try to imagine how you yourself would feel if you were in their shoes.

You will probably be able to pick up all kinds of subtle hints about what is going on behind the mask that the person seems to be wearing. If you can't pick up such clues when the conversation is actually taking place, you can always replay it in your mind, as a film editor replays a film, to look for clues you might have missed the first time around.

Dr. Susan Frank, formerly of Yale University, did some very interesting research on how students picked up varieties and nuances of expression they might have missed, by replaying conversations and other scenes in their minds. She had several students assemble for sessions once a week to share their daydreams and night dreams (of which they had kept records). The students were not expected to interpret or analyze these dreams—just to tell them. After ten weeks Dr. Frank gave the students tests to measure their capacity for empathy: the ability to understand what another person was feeling, through observing that person's facial expressions. She found that members of the group who had practiced this daydream and night dream awareness were significantly more empathic than a control group which had not been asked to do such exercises. She also found that a number of student actors in the Yale Drama School who were doing these kinds of exercises to help develop their acting skills had also improved their ability to empathize and to understand the feelings of others. Actually, the whole school of method acting is based on this premise.

It seems as if in the fantasies and the daydreams and night dreams stored in our heads there lies information that we can use to sharpen our sensitivity to the feelings and moods of others and to the subtleties of verbal conversation. How can you make the best use of this technique?

127

To sum up, you can replay in your mind situations that involved a person with whom you find it difficult to communicate, as we have indicated.

Let's assume you have an employee whose responses baffle you. For some reason, he or she seems colder and more distant than would seem normal under the circumstances. You would like to establish a better working relationship, but you don't know whether the employee is just a generally unresponsive person or whether you are doing or saying something that chills the atmosphere. Try recalling, as clearly as possible, three or four occasions on which you have been puzzled by this person's unresponsiveness. Play these scenes over and over in your mind. You may find a clue that you missed earlier during the actual situation.

One of the authors of this book had such a problem with an editor. The editor kept commissioning her articles, so the problem clearly was not that she felt the author incompetent. However, a general pall seemed to settle on all conversations about work that needed to be done. Both parties were clearly uncomfortable with each other. While she was replaying these scenes in her mind, it became evident to the writer that much of that coldness became apparent whenever the fact that she would have to commute to New York from Connecticut was mentioned. Did the editor harbor prejudices against commuters? Had she had a particularly bad experience with a resident of Connecticut? Since the editor was a particularly bright and competent young woman, it seemed unlikely that she would even subconsciously, hold on to such a petty prejudice. The writer finally decided, after replaying several of the incidents in her mind, to come right out and ask the editor what the problem was. The editor was surprised by the question; she had not really been aware of her lack of warmth. But she too went over the relationship carefully, and came to the conclusion that she had been indeed prejudiced, not against commuters or

128 Connecticut residents, but against writers who

worked at their craft part-time and whose main interests seemed to center around their families. Reasonably or unreasonably, she felt that writers who were also suburban homemakers were to be taken less seriously than full-time career women. On talking the situation over, she realized that she had not been entirely fair. After all, she was commissioning the writer to do articles on a fairly regular basis; the work was satisfactorily done and came in on the deadline. Actually, she admitted, she was probably a bit envious of the freedom freelancers enjoy, whether they live in the suburbs or not. This confrontation and the conversation that followed were the beginning of a whole new relationship. The two women are friends now and the writer hopes that the editor will reexamine her reactions to other free-lancers who may or may not live in suburban Connecticut.

Only after replaying the scenes with the editor several times was the writer able to put her finger on the puzzling problem area in the relationship.

Similar techniques would probably be even more valuable in more intimate relationships. For instance, many husbands and wives engage in what might be called "revolving door" fights. One minute they are getting along fine, and the next they find themselves in a heated argument, often about some seemingly unimportant matter. In replaying these scenes in their minds, they may be able to spot some common thread in the events leading up to the fight. Most people have a few very sensitive areas. Perhaps either or both touched such an area before the argument erupted. Let's say the husband is particularly sensitive about his professional accomplishments, especially when they are compared with those of his brother. A perfectly harmless remark by the wife that her sister-in-law called her that morning and that the brother had received another promotion might be the beginning of a nasty fight. The husband sees the remark as an attack on his own accomplishments and counters with a suggestion that his wife (who is particularly **129** sensitive about her figure) seems to have gained a lot of weight lately. Now she feels attacked. The situation can only go downhill from there. But in replaying the scene in their minds both can learn to pinpoint which sensitive spots had better not be brought up early in the evening or late at night, and a lot of misunderstanding can be avoided.

In Ingmar Bergman's *Scenes from a Marriage,* a couple is seen subtly rubbing each other's sensitivities raw. Neither seems to understand what is happening. When the husband, apparently without explanation, decides to leave his wife for another woman, she is surprised and devastated. She had not for a second suspected such an involvement, and, strange as it may seem, he is just as surprised as she is. He does not understand what went wrong with their seemingly perfect marriage. He just knows he feels suffocated and wants to leave. Only after both begin to rethink and replay what went on during the many years they were married (this does not happen until the last episode, long after they are divorced and have married other partners) are they able to analyze what stresses and insecurities broke them up in the first place. This seven-hour television series came to the United States for the first time as a 90-minute film. Many people who saw the film did not understand why the couple broke up. When the husband told his wife that he was leaving her, everyone in the audience was as surprised as she was; there had been no hint of dissatisfaction, and the whole problem seemed totally irrational. The much longer film as it was shown on TV carefully developed the hidden conflicts between the marriage partners; then the husband's action no longer seemed unmotivated—callous perhaps, but not unreasonable.

In real life, clues to conflicts are obviously present. Nobody is cutting our past down from seven hours to 90 minutes. But we may have to look at what has been happening again and again to make sense of seemingly senseless interpersonal problems.

After you have spotted the problems in a relationship, you might try out new and different approaches through fantasy.

Imagine alternative ways of approaching the situation. Play them over several times in your mind. Set up the scene as you would if you were directing a film or a television show. What actions tend to produce what reactions? If the reaction is consistently negative, perhaps your action should be changed.

Psychiatrists and psychologists have used this kind of mind theatre to help patients cope with seemingly unsolvable problems. Some use psychodrama, in which some patients play themselves and other patients play figures who are close to the patient and with whom the relationship is strained. Everybody acts out scenes that may have occurred in real life. In that way, they are able to analyze what went wrong in the first place, and in another imaginary scene, try to set it right.

Assertiveness training seminars, which are very popular these days, use a similar technique. People who are unable to make their wishes known to others are asked to imagine themselves in a series of carefully structured scenarios. An employer who can't tell an employee that a mistake has been made may be asked to set up a scene in which he or she tells that employee that the job was unsatisfactory and has to be done over. Or a woman who finds it impossible to tell her mother that she would rather go skiing for Thanksgiving than come home as always for Thanksgiving dinner is asked to set up a scene in which she tactfully but firmly advises her parent that this year she's going to Stowe, Vermont. People who participate in the assertiveness training seminars are often asked to play these scenes in three ways:

1. In their usual nonassertive manner.
2. In a hostile, aggressive manner.
3. In a constructive, productive, assertive posture.

131

They are asked to watch their body language, the tones of their voices, and so on, and they begin to learn that even a completely reasonable statement may turn out to be self-defeating if it is used in an angry, hurt way, or an apologetic, hesitant tone.

The trainer for these groups hopes that eventually the participants will become sensitive enough to their own actions and to the reactions of those with whom they are attempting to communicate, to stop being everyone's doormat, but without becoming Attila the Hun, either.

If you find it impossible to show feelings, you might try to show more emotion first in your daydreams and fantasies to help yourself become more comfortable with this kind of openness.

If you are a fairly uptight person, you have probably already run into all kinds of misunderstandings with people close to you. At first it may seem impossible to break ingrained habits of a lifetime, but eventually you may not find it at all impossible to become more open and warmer in real-life situations.

Imagine yourself in a situation in which you would have liked to show emotion but were unable to do so comfortably. Then, in your mind, play the situation over, this time allowing your feelings to surface in your expression as well as in your words.

At first you may think this kind of approach is somewhat phony. After all, aren't we all looking for authenticity in our actions and feelings? But that is exactly the point. If you cannot show what you feel, you are depriving yourself and the people you love of some rich and rewarding experiences. In a way, you were disguising your true self when you could not show how you felt. If you practice letting others know what is going on inside of you, you'll find that your relationships become more honest, even if occasionally you show such negative emotions as anger or fear. You will find that you will also be able to allow love and joy to come to

132

the surface—and all in all, you will probably find that others are more, not less, comfortable with you. You will certainly feel more comfortable with yourself.

Sexuality
and Fantasy

Almost everybody fantasizes about sex. Some people enjoy these fantasies and encourage them. Others tend to push them out of their minds. Still others feel intensely guilty about them. Psychiatrists listen to a lot of sexual fantasies, and so do priests in the confessional. Some of the world's greatest works of art, such as Japanese water colors, Indian temple images, and pre-Columbian sculptures, are based on sexual mind imagery—and so is some of the worst trash seen on the porno strips of some of our large cities. There seems to be a special affinity in our civilization between fantasy and sexuality.

This is not difficult to understand. Children, long before adolescence, love such sensual experiences as touching and rubbing. Before they are regularly capable of experiencing those specific genital sensations that adults feel, they are absorbing a great deal of material about the power of sexuality and the beauty and excitement of romantic relationships from TV, magazines, books, movies, and rock lyrics. Girls especially begin to fantasize early on about getting married and setting up housekeeping.

136 Barbie and Ken, America's most popular dress-up

dolls, come with complete bridal outfits. In spite of our so-called sexual revolution, the details of sexuality and of all this romance and glamour remain something of a mystery to most children. They don't have some of the physical sensations of sex in "the right places," and they are often quite ignorant about the nature of sexual intercourse. Therefore, sexuality, from early childhood on, has a mysterious and enticing quality—exactly the kind of quality that daydreams are made of.

Besides getting from the media sexual hints, along with somewhat ambiguous information, children often engage in sex play with each other. From playing "doctor" in the garage, Susie and Timmy learn something about the differences between male and female anatomy, but they can still only guess at what these differences will mean to them later on when the game turns into reality. It's no wonder that realizing there's something out there that everybody considers important and delightful (and that adults don't seem to want to discuss in any detail) causes youngsters to try to supplement the actual information they have received with very special, private, and persistent sexual daydreams.

By the time they grow into early adolescence, many of them masturbate while fantasizing. What they are doing is systematically reinforcing their daydreams with the reward of sexual pleasure. Sexual fantasies thus hold an unusually important and significant role in most people's development. Since the young children have no experience and little information about sexual matters, their fantasies can become exceedingly strange, even bizarre. All of this is completely normal and natural. Some of these odd fantasies even continue into adult life.

In his practice, one of the co-authors has met patients who daydream about sex with men (or women) from outer space, with partners who beat and torture them, with TV and motion picture personalities, and with other highly unlikely partners. For our purposes, we shall limit ourselves to the more common, everyday fantasies that the vast majority of reasonably normal individuals may experience.

A patient, whom we shall call Sally, described to one of the co-authors a fantasy that she had regularly during sexual relations with her husband. Her confession came toward the end of her psychoanalytic treatment and the therapist was somewhat taken aback by this new information, since it had seemed to him that the therapy had gone well and that she was about ready for termination of treatment. Sally reported that each time she made love to her husband she would not become sufficiently aroused to reach orgasm unless she developed a fantasy that she was being held prisoner by the secret police in a Communist country. As her captors held her tied down, they stripped off her clothes and proceeded, one after another, to rape her. This fantasy stimulated her to the point that she was able to reach orgasm easily. When she kept herself from letting these images float through her mind, lovemaking was much less thrilling.

When the author heard this story, he became seriously concerned that perhaps he might have missed some basic problem of masochism underlying Sally's psychology. But she seemed to be doing well in her daily life and insisted that she was deeply in love with her husband, who loved her in return and was a perfectly competent sexual partner. She was sure that it was not anything that he did or failed to do that made it necessary for her to develop her rather strange fantasy. She's had these particular mind images ever since puberty, she said, and during those years they were often associated with erotic self-stimulation of some kind.

As the author explored the situation further, it became clear to him that Sally, who had been raised very strictly and was taught to feel ashamed of sexual impulses as a young girl, had to stage these violent scenes in her mind. In effect, her fantasy allowed her to let herself go. She could do this because she was doing so involuntarily; she was at
the mercy of others.

In this way, the fantasy had become so strongly associated with the development of strong erotic sensations that she could not give it up even when she was able to have real and very satisfying sexual intercourse with her gentle, loving husband. She continued to call up these images of violence which were completely unknown to her husband, while he was delighted that he was able to stimulate and satisfy her so completely. She did not tell him, because she was too embarrassed to do so, but she wondered whether she should try to give up her Communist captors while in bed with her mate. After extensive analysis of all the possible implications of these fantasies there seemed to be no overwhelming reason why she should not indulge in them from time to time if they helped her to reach orgasm. It seemed like just one more useful way in which imagination could further the pleasure of human experience.

Subsequently the author began to look deeper into the question of how many women had developed some kind of adolescent sexual fantasies that helped them, as adults, to heighten sexual arousal and to reach orgasm during sexual intercourse. Psychoanalytical literature mentions many such instances and tends to interpret them as being a sign that the woman wants to be forced or dominated by the man. "When rape becomes inevitable, lie back and enjoy it," is the kind of statement that has been influenced by this thinking—and it is naturally and correctly abhorrent to most women. Rape fantasies have often been treated as signs of deep-seated problems with neurotic masochism or as indications of penis envy.

Sally's story prompted the author to question whether such fantasies were necessarily neurotic. After all, she was having a mature and satisfying relationship with a man she loved, and her mind images didn't seem to get in the way.

The author decided to collaborate on a research project with one of his former students, Dr. Barbara Hariton. They would attempt to find out **139** how widespread the occurrence of fantasies during sexual intercourse was among normal married women. Dr. Hariton interviewed and submitted questionnaires to approximately 150 suburban wives and found that about two-thirds of them had fairly frequent fantasies while having intercourse with their husbands. These fantasies included images of being with a completely different lover, often a man of their acquaintance, or having a famous personality in bed with them (at the time, Paul Newman led the list), or having mind pictures similar to Sally's: being forced into submission by robbers, Nazis, or Communists, or being sold as harem girls required to submit to the whims of a sultan. The power of such fantasies is obviously still present; witness the popularity of a movie such as *King Kong*, in which the heroine is wooed by a 40-foot gorilla.

As the researchers looked over their results, they found that many of the women who had fantasies about being forced to submit sexually or of being dominated by powerful men were usually neither deeply neurotic nor submissive nor dependent persons in their daily lives. These fantasies, like Sally's, often started during adolescence, when a young girl is still ambivalent about her sexual feelings. Often she is confused about the propriety of the feelings she is experiencing, and often she is influenced by the kind of adventure stories and monster movies she sees which put women into this kind of a submissive position.

It's not at all unusual for a girl who is already stimulated by such material to reinforce her erotic feelings with masturbation or other forms of self-stimulation. Many of these girls grow up with fairly clear encapsulated fantasies that are closely associated with sexual arousal. The fantasies do not necessarily, or even usually, relate to the men they know in real life. Actually, the opposite may be true. The co-author's experience has been that many women with forceful personalities who compete with men in business and the professions are embarrassed about the fact that they have persistent fantasies about being harem girls or prostitutes. Such fantasies *can* occasionally cause some sexual problems, but only if the woman feels that her mind images are wrong and bad, and so tries to avoid the fantasies or inhibit her sexual response.

In psychotherapy with such a woman it is often necessary to help her to recognize that her fantasy is harmless; it doesn't mean she's suddenly turned into a masochist or a clinging vine. The best thing she can do in such a situation is to regard her floating images as exactly what they are: pleasurable fantasies that help her achieve sexual gratification.

Sex therapists have taken this position more and more. They may attempt to discover what sexual fantasies husbands and wives have; however, they do so not to suppress or change the mind images, but to reassure couples with problems that fantasies are normal and may often be very useful in allowing men and women to shed their sexual inhibitions.

Even though research has been focused more on the sexual fantasies of women, men have them too, of course. In the male they also usually start during adolescence, and may take some odd forms.

Another of the co-author's students, Dr. Anthony Campagna, explored the nature and extent of masturbation fantasies reported by Yale University freshmen. It seems that many of these young men had fantasies about women they knew, including some with whom they had actually had intercourse. Students who did not have a great deal of sexual experience, on the other hand, had more fantastic mind images. Some fantasized that they were motion picture producers with "casting couches," used to bed down a variety of exceedingly attractive young starlets. There's a male version of the harem daydream too, with the man forcing one or more of his many wives and concubines to have sex with him. Men who were able to produce elaborate and picturesque fantasies were usually those who were able to show a good deal of imagination in other areas of their lives too.

Another, less imaginative group of young men

were more likely to have daydreams in which all they could see was a portion of a woman's body, or at least a faceless person, whom they could not identify. Sometimes the imaginary partner would be a prostitute or a waitress they had seen briefly in a local restaurant. Occasionally, a student produced a pattern of daydreams in which the sexual activity was deviant from the norm: homosexual encounters, or sexual activities with extremely unusual partners.

The interesting fact that emerged from all of this research, however, is that despite the great range of fantasies, only the pattern of the faceless fantasy was apparently related to indications of emotional disturbance. In other words, sexual fantasy can have many different kinds of characters and plot lines, including some fairly extravagant ones, without being an indication of a deep or severe psychological problem. Only when an individual starts to put some of these more bizarre fantasies to work in real life need one be concerned about his or her mental health.

For instance, professional intervention is clearly indicated if an individual feels that he or she must bind up a partner in chains, or inflict pain on that partner, or allow the partner to mistreat him or her. Most people's fantasies, even though they may contain some rather strange components, remain at the level of thought, and can simply be a means of pleasurable self-entertainment or heightened arousal.

Sex therapists have found a number of very practical uses for fantasy to enhance sexual experience or to help inhibited sexual partners overcome various blocks and other difficulties. While our purpose in this book is not to provide a complete guide to the great range of techniques that have been developed during the past few years to help men and women enjoy full and satisfying sexual experience, we do have some suggestions about how fantasy can be used to treat sexual problems and also to help the average person increase sexual pleasure

and variety.

Performance anxiety

In her book *The New Sex Therapy*, Dr. Helen Singer Kaplan calls attention to the fact that many sex problems begin because one or both of the partners pay too much attention to the actual sensation they experience in the genitals and deliberately go about trying to increase these sensations, as if they were in some sort of erotic competition. A man who constantly thinks of the presence, absence, or extent of his erection may find that his penis grows limp before long. A woman who is tense because she's afraid she won't have an orgasm may very well be unable to have one. All of this is known as "spectatoring": the participants seem to stand outside of themselves watching and judging the way they perform. From what we know about the biofeedback effects of our own thoughts upon autonomic responses, it is not surprising that the negative feelings aroused by such "performance anxiety" can be devastating.

Over the years, men especially have learned to use distracting fantasies so that they will not be so conscious of their own erections, feelings of excitement, and so on. Many of these fantasies are non-erotic (like visualizing sales charts at the office or thinking about baseball scores). Men do this to be sure that they can maintain an erection long enough to bring their partners to climax. We can find an excellent example of this in yet another Woody Allen movie. In *Play It Again, Sam*, the hero has gone to bed for the first time with his best friend's wife. In the morning the couple share their good feelings. The woman says to Woody: "You were really wonderful, but did you have to keep saying, 'Slide, Willie Mays, Slide!' when you were reaching your climax?" Women, who often have slower sexual responses, usually do not concern themselves with holding back their erotic feelings in this way. However, in either case, according to Dr. Kaplan and to Masters and Johnson, this kind of distracting behavior is undesirable.

In many instances, an erotic fantasy, often a holdover from adolescent mind images, would be **143** more effective in distracting men from their focus on the genital area and their worries about climaxing too soon. Women who have special difficulties in reaching orgasm might well be encouraged to use similar techniques to distract them from their own version of performance anxiety.

Using fantasies in real life

Many people don't have performance anxieties and don't need this kind of extra stimulation. But couples often have very different rhythms and backgrounds. Even though they may love each other, their long separate histories of fantasies about sex may inhibit them from making their mutual experiences more rewarding. Sometimes, especially when the fantasy seems a little peculiar, one partner may have a problem confiding in the other. Dr. Kaplan, in her book *The New Sex Therapy*, tells of one young man who could not consummate his marriage of more than six months to a woman with whom he was deeply in love. In the course of treatment, he confided to the therapist that he had developed a fantasy in childhood which associated sexual arousal and climax with a picture of himself as Superman. Often he actually wore a red cape as an adolescent when engaged in self-stimulation. Rather than being alarmed by this story, the therapist simply encouraged the couple to act out the fantasy together, as part of the other homework exercises they were given to increase sexual responsiveness. Much to the couple's surprise, the use of the fantasy, even without the red cape, produced considerable excitement and allowed the couple to make love for the first time.

Sharing sexual fantasies

Sharing sexual fantasies can actually be a helpful part of lovemaking. Some couples enjoy acting out some of these fantasies. One couple enjoyed playing "seduced and seducer" in which the husband would "lure" his wife, often fully dressed, to bed with caresses and compliments. This kind of

144

thing is not always necessary, of course, but it can add a lot of fun and variety. Readers of Marabel Morgan's *Total Woman* are encouraged to dress up in all kinds of exotic costumes: wearing nothing but Saran Wrap and a red bow, or baby doll pajamas and a cowboy hat to keep up their husbands' flagging interest. This sexual prescription may be one of the reasons why the book maintains its position on the paperback best seller list, and its author her position as a popular talk show guest.

Using fantasies as a clue to other problems

Fantasy can often be a useful clue when some things seem to be going wrong in a sexual relationship. Paying special attention to patterns of daydreams and recurring fantasies, sexual or otherwise, may point the way to the cause of whatever is happening. In one case, a young woman found herself completely unresponsive to a man she liked a lot. She was, however, aware of recurring daydreams in which she saw herself being ravished by a semihuman monster who looked a little like the statue of a Greek satyr she had seen in an art book. This fantasy did not please her; it frightened her instead. She did not have it during the sexual act, but she noticed that her lover had a peculiar habit of sniffling and breathing through his mouth, because of a sinus condition, when he became aroused. She realized that this recurring mannerism, of which her lover was quite unaware, somehow tied in with the monster fantasy which embarrassed and scared her. When she finally was able to tell her therapist, and eventually her lover, about this, the young man was able to exert some control over his peculiar breathing, and their love life progressed in a satisfactory manner.

Another young woman kept a record of her daydreams and night dreams, at the suggestion of her therapist, because she was having some severe sexual problem with her lover, who was a fellow student at a school of social work. It became evident from reading her journal entries that in her

145

earliest childhood she had been exposed to some semiseductive experiences with her uncle, and from this she had formed a fantasy that cast her in the role of the "magic helper" of an older man, who would take her out of her squalid and impoverished real-life situation. Although she took steps to improve her own position by working hard in school, eventually winning a fellowship to graduate school, she still fantasized unconsciously about a May-December relationship in which an older, richer man would rescue and take care of her. The young man with whom she was having the love affair was neither old nor rich. He wasn't even very ambitious, and would probably never earn any more money than she would.

After she discovered what had been bothering her, she had to make up her mind whether she wanted to give up the present relationship to wait for her elderly prince in shining armor, or whether she wanted to stay with her present lover. As it turned out, she decided that although her fantasies were certainly not realistic, there were some real problems with her young man. His lack of ambition and drive would probably continue to bother her. Eventually she completed the work toward her degree, became a moderately successful social worker, and married a somewhat older and prosperous engineer. He wasn't exactly what she dreamed about—but he was a lot closer to her fantasy than her former lover.

Damaging fantasies in real life

Many people try to carry their fantasies into real life and that can cause a good deal of damage. A great many middle-aged men daydream about meeting and having affairs with women who are considerably younger than their wives. Having this kind of affair in your head (or lusting in your heart) will probably cause very little damage. Trying for the real thing might. In the first place, breaking up a long-standing marriage for a will-of-the-wisp fantasy has rarely brought happiness to anyone.

Second, a daydream translated into real life can often turn out to be a nightmare. John Powers, whom we met in Chapter 1, had just that experience when he began an affair with his young, attractive secretary. When his wife found out and threatened divorce, he realized that he never should have tried to solve his middle-age crisis in this manner. He had not enjoyed the affair very much and he and his secretary had little in common, except sex. But now that his indiscretion was threatening his marriage, he realized that he actually preferred sitting in front of the TV with a cold beer to making the discotheques with his much younger companion. He had had a need to prove to himself that he could still be attractive to a younger woman. But even this wish was not realistic: the chances are the secretary agreed to the affair not because she found him irresistible, but *because* of his age and status. She was fulfilling some kind of fantasy of her own (similar to the one experienced by the social worker) and, in real life, she had not found the situation any more to her liking than he had to his.

On the whole, then, fantasy and imagination can be invaluable in enriching your sex life and making it more varied and enjoyable. The trick is not to allow yourself to forget the difference between dreams and reality, between acting out your fantasy inside your head and allowing it to cross the border into your actual daily life.

How to Tell
when Your Fantasies
May Harm You

Recently a college student wrote to a popular newspaper advice columnist to tell her of a persistent fantasy that bothered him a great deal. While supposedly studying his textbook or taking lecture notes, he was actually forming vivid pictures in his mind, all concerned with killing one or more of his fellow students in a variety of picturesque and bloody ways. He indicated that he had had this problem for quite some time and wondered whether he should discuss it with someone. The columnist, quite correctly, advised the young man to see his family physician for a referral to a good psychiatrist as quickly as possible. Everybody occasionally has fantasies about eliminating a particularly obnoxious colleague or relative, she pointed out. But such persistent mental images were a sign of a clear and present danger. The young man might never actually put his violent fantasies into practice, but he almost surely was experiencing symptoms of an emotional problem with which he should be dealing promptly. And good professional help was imperative.

There are some good historical precedents for the columnist's warning and advice. For instance,

Sirhan Sirhan, the man who shot Robert Kennedy, had kept a diary in which he pictured over and over again in his imagination exactly the kind of scene which he eventually enacted. Arthur Bremer, the man who shot Governor George Wallace, had a similar diary. The FBI found it when the agents went through the would-be assassin's room. John Wilkes Booth, the second-rate actor who shot Abraham Lincoln, had two kinds of fantasies. One pictured him to be a superb, successful actor like his brother, Edwin, whom he admired and envied, and the other cast him as the "hero" who would finally bring victory to the South by assassinating the President. If he had been able to realize his first fantasy, he might never have realized his second, and the history of the United States would have been very different.

There are other kinds of fantasies besides murderous ones which might indicate an emotional problem. For instance, there is the absent-minded professor. He forgets to bring home the mushrooms his wife needs for her dinner party, continuously looks for his glasses which are usually firmly set on his nose all the time, does not remember that his grades for Roman History II are due at the Dean's office on Monday (he may even have mislaid the examination papers altogether), and generally spends his life in a haze of problems—all because his mind wanders to more pleasant locations than his wife's kitchen or his rather boring Roman History class.

Susan Williams is not a professor of history. She *was* a secretary in a computer firm, her third job in four years. Everybody likes her. She is a pleasant, attractive, intelligent young woman. The only trouble is that she forgets things, and what she does not forget, she loses. Her employers had put up with a certain amount of inconvenience but, like all the others, they regretfully decided that they would have to dispense with her services if they wished to keep the office minimally efficient.

Susan's problem is that she spends most of **151**

her time in a fantasy world which is a great deal more interesting than her mundane office. In her own head, she floats around a charming Mediterranean village (she had once seen some interesting slides of Monte Carlo) dressed like Cher. If she pictures herself making a living in her mental hideaway, she doesn't consider typing and filing. Either she is occupied weaving exotic clothes out of native yarns, or she is sitting in a delightful little coffee house singing folk songs to the accompaniment of a guitar. Since she can neither weave nor sing, and the employment compensation on which she frequently lives is not enough to pay for a trip to Indianapolis, much less Monte Carlo, she never really attempts to put her daydreams into practice. When she was fired from the computer firm, she decided to take stock of herself to see what she might do about her absent-minded daydreams.

She decided to give herself a mind signal every time she floated off to her Mediterranean village. And she scheduled some regular hours (not between nine and five Mondays through Fridays) in which she could indulge in her daydreams. In her new job, she stops herself from fantasizing when she should be typing. She still slips up occasionally; last week she filed her pay check and took an inventory report to the bank to cash. But, considering her pleasant personality and her many other attractions, it looks as if she can keep her present job as long as she wishes. She is saving her extra money in a special vacation account which she hopes will eventually get her to Monaco, and she is taking guitar lessons—just in case. The point of Susan's story is that healthy fantasies have their own stop-and-go mechanisms built in. A person does not *have* to daydream when he or she should be working or paying attention to some other important aspect of life. Daydreaming at inappropriate times is self-indulgence, quite similar to constantly eating too many luscious whipped cream desserts. It takes some practice to learn to use fantasy (as we pointed out in Chapter 3). It also takes some practice and some will power to stop using it at inopportune moments.

Then there are those who try to translate some overambitious fantasy scheme into reality. Again, there are some good historical examples of this kind of fantasy activity. Napoleon fantasized that somehow he would inspire his troops to march across the icy winter steppes of Russia to conquer the Tsar's army on their own ground. His generals warned him that this was a highly impractical scheme and would most probably lead to disaster. Napoleon, who had been able to make a few other unlikely fantasies come true, refused to listen. The generals turned out to be right.

Hitler, with Napoleon's example before him, insisted on repeating the experiment. His generals, too, told him that attacking Russia in the winter, while Great Britain still remained undefeated, would be a terrible error. Hitler was convinced that his fantasies were more real than the hard logic of his generals. Of course, he turned out to be wrong, too—but he carried his daydreams even further than Napoleon: he accused the generals of being traitors who refused to commit troops and heavy artillery they were holding in reserve to the battle. The problem with that reasoning was that there were no reserve troops or guns. They existed only in Hitler's mind, as Albert Speer, one of his few personal confidants, explained in his book, *The Spandau Diaries*. Some psycho-historians now believe that Hitler was certifiably mad—that he actually saw and heard objects and people that were, in fact, not there. Others believe that Hitler's fantasy life came close enough to reality so that he firmly believed that if he only insisted, he could force those around him to make anything he wanted come true. After all, who would have thought that an ugly, undersized, badly educated corporal, who was not even a German, would one day lead German armies to victories over half the civilized world?

Not many of us have our minds set on conquering half the world. More commonly, we

153

would just like to conquer those four individuals who stand in our way to the next promotion, or that inconsiderate banker who tells us that the mortgage we need to buy the house we want is too large for our income, or our mother-in-law who tells us that our noodle pudding, or our job potential, is just not up to snuff. And a certain amount of harmless mental gymnastics don't hurt. We might well imagine that those four job competitors have all decided to move to Australia, that the banker has suddenly discovered that our elderly uncle is about to leave us a million dollars, or that our mother-in-law has just burned her noodle pudding. That kind of fantasy will help to get us over our frustrated ambitions more quickly, and allow us to deal with our real-life problems more constructively. But some of us may actually tell ourselves persistently that something desirable is going to happen simply because we want it to. Along that road lies danger.

Take Maximilian Jones, for instance. Perhaps because of his rather grandiose name, he has always been sure that the future would turn out the way he wished it to, regardless of what he himself contributed to such a result. In spite of rather mediocre grades in high school, he was convinced that his college entrance examinations would be so brilliant that he would surely be accepted at Harvard. He even convinced his parents that this would undoubtedly happen. Of course, it did not. His college boards turned out to be pretty much on a par with his high school grades. He was disappointed, but decided to attend a local community college, convinced that he would do so well within a year that he would be able to transfer to Harvard, or any other school he chose. He finished in the top half of the community college class, but that was just not good enough to qualify him for Harvard. By now his parents had decided that Maximilian just was not Ivy League material, and they were perfectly happy to have him graduate from the institution of learning he was presently attending with a respectable grade average. But not Maximilian. He dreamed every semester that the great breakthrough was imminent and that soon he would be on his way, academically speaking. He continued this pattern after he graduated from the community college. He applied for jobs for which he was completely unqualified, firmly expecting to be hired. He courted a young woman who had plainly shown her interest in his cousin, an Ivy League college graduate. He expected promotions which were never within his reach and raises which were out of keeping with the company's policies.

His wife, a sensible young woman whom he had had the good luck to marry after the first woman married his cousin, worried that the repeated disappointments would eventually sour Maximilian's character and disposition. She also felt that he was not realizing perfectly achievable goals because he was constantly reaching for unachievable ones. She has urged him to get some psychological goal counseling to find out why he does not seem able to face his real-life limitations. So far he has refused. Perhaps one day, one of his persistent disappointments will drive him into a real depression. In that case, therapy may no longer be a matter of choice, but of necessity.

Susan and Maximilian had their own private daydream and fantasy problems, but there are a few that many of us share, perhaps as a part of our social and cultural heritage. Let's take just two: The Romantic Marriage Daydream and the Horatio Alger Myth.

The Romantic Marriage Daydream (hereafter referred to as RMD) probably has its roots in our very early childhood. Little girls encounter in their first storybooks beautiful maidens who meet handsome, and by implication, also rich, princes. Barbie and Ken dolls come with complete wedding outfits. Little boys are not exposed quite as consistently and frequently to RMD, but they seem to absorb it, too, somewhere along the line. At any rate, by the time both sexes reach the teen years, they have

155

usually come to share the fantasy that somehow, somewhere, they will meet the perfect mate, get married, and live happily ever after. There are many dangerous aspects to this particular community fantasy, as borne out by the ever-increasing statistics on divorce and separation. As part of the fantasy, many of us tend to believe that love conquers all, that couples unsuited to each other by emotional makeup or family background will somehow become a happy pair because they are in love. The rescue fantasy of the young woman who marries a heavy drinker or gambler hoping to "change" him is another example of the unrealistic RMD.

The origins of RMD are peculiarly American. Europeans also enjoy fairy tales and romantic novels, but somehow they don't seem to take them quite so literally. And certainly some of the best British novelists make it crystal clear that a happy marriage is possible only if the would-be partners are emotionally, socially, and even financially suited to each other. In a typical Jane Austen novel a practical, intelligent young heroine might *think* she is in love with a penniless scoundrel. Elizabeth Bennett in *Pride and Prejudice*, for instance, considers falling in love with Mr. Wickham, a typically bad egg on both moral and financial grounds, but thinks better of it and marries Mr. Darcy, a man of high moral character with an income of more than 10,000 pounds per year. Elizabeth's feckless sister Lydia marries the abominable Wickham and, of course, lives unhappily and penniless ever after.

In a slightly different context, Charles Dickens's David Copperfield marries the lovely but childish and incompetent Dora. There is no doubt that the marriage would have turned out disastrously (similar marriages in other Dickens novels do), but Dora, luckily, succumbs to a romantically vague wasting disease, leaving David free to marry the highly suitable, very practical and competent Agnes, and thus presumably lives happily ever after too.

Even in modern British stories love does not conquer all, particularly if there are differences of class, standards, and financial position. Remember the marriage of James Bellamy, the son and heir of the aristocratic upstairs family in the TV series *Upstairs, Downstairs* to middle-class Hazel? A total disaster, although the script writer made it clear that at the beginning of their relationship both were very much in love; they persisted in getting married in spite of objections from both sets of families and the whole Bellamy downstairs staff, particularly the butler and the cook, Mrs. Bridges (who in the last episode of the series very suitably marry each other).

In German and French literature, ill-assorted pairs of lovers tend to die for love, but they hardly ever marry each other and live happily ever after. Our European cousins are much too realistic for such an assumption.

Oriental countries have their own form of RMD: fairy tales of beautiful, unsuitable maidens and handsome princes almost always end tragically. The family disapproves and there is no wedding. Instead there is a double suicide. In real life, a surprisingly large number of marriages in many Asian and African cultures are still arranged by the two families.

We don't know whether anyone has ever done a good sociological or anthropological study of the matter, but it seems to us that RMD most often results in households headed by single females, as the U.S. Census Bureau so unromantically puts it.

But clergymen, lawyers, and marriage counselors who see many distressed couples tell us that our collective fantasy of the perfect romantic marriage wrecks many perfectly acceptable relationships. The couple, after the first glow of the honeymoon has worn off, thinks that something essential is missing and that the whole enterprise is probably one large mistake. Out there, somewhere, is the perfect partner. The lady or the gentleman on the other side of the bed must be lacking in some essen-

157

tial quality, because, if he or she were not, living happily ever after would be possible. Men and women may spend their whole lives looking for that perfect mate who does not exist. More realistic couples accept each other, realizing that even the most beautiful piece of art will probably contain a few flaws (it may actually be the flaws that make the difference between art and computer programming), and that all relationships require some anger and some hurt to be human. Tolstoy said that all happy families are alike but that every unhappy marriage is different from every other. That's a dubious statement at best, but in one sense it is true. Couples who are happily married rarely share the "we'll live happily ever after, without problems and fights as long as we both shall live" daydream.

Now about that Horatio Alger Fantasy, hereafter referred to as HAF. During the late nineteenth century an American hack writer, Horatio Alger, produced a series of novels with very similar plots. They concerned some poor but honest and hardworking young men who started out at the bottom of the educational, financial, and professional ladder and worked themselves up to becoming presidents of banks, department stores, manufacturing industries, and other respectable and lucrative organizations.

The Horatio Alger books were aimed at the teenage trade. Parents bought these novels for their sons in the hope that the sons would want to emulate these brilliant career accomplishments. Hardly anyone reads the novels anymore. For one thing, they were very badly written, and for another, most of today's teenagers would consider the characters hokey. However, the idea behind those novels, which obviously predated their author by a couple of centuries, has remained with us. Any poor but honest young man (and in the era of Equal Opportunity legislation, any poor but honest young woman) can become President of General Motors, or for that matter, President of the New York Stock Exchange or of the United States, through constant and single-minded application to hard work.

158

This is a fairly harmless fantasy on the surface, but it also has its negative side: any poor but honest young man or woman who does not make it to the presidency of one or all of the above just isn't trying hard enough. Carried to a further extreme, it results in an even more damaging fantasy: blaming the victim. If you remain poor and unsuccessful, it's because you missed out on all those unlimited opportunities for improving yourself, and therefore your lack of success is your own fault.

But if we look at the actual plots of the Horatio Alger novels, this kind of interpretation falls apart, even at the author's very simple level. All those poor but honest young men did indeed spend their evenings reading self-improvement tracts and studying acounting (instead of amusing themselves at the neighborhood bar), but their rise to fame and fortune actually began with one seemingly unrelated event that can only be classified as exteme good luck. One Horatio Alger hero rescued his employer's daughter from a runaway horse and her father was so grateful that he promoted him on the spot from office boy to a much higher position. What's more, the young man eventually married the daughter—and all of us know that there's nothing like having the boss for a father-in-law to ensure quick advancement. Other heroes prevented hold-ups and robberies, rescued kidnapped grand-children, and generally distinguished themselves in ways that had very little to do with office management and efficiency. They were rewarded, or at least noticed, because of one act of bravery. After that, it was uphill all the way, career-wise.

In real life, such opportunities for instant heroism rarely happen. And what's more, a lot of very good people who work hard and behave honestly do not become corporation presidents, become internationally famous brain surgeons, or win the Pulitzer Prize for literature. Many a young reporter may dream of becoming a Woodward or Bernstein; many a young actress may fantasize herself as Liv Ullman; many would-be scientists may dream of becoming Dr. Jonas Salk, but there's ob-

159

viously only so much room at the top, and most of us lead perfectly normal, reasonably happy lives without reaching impossible career and personal goals. It's not our fault, and there's very little point in blaming ourselves if we are doing the best we can.

So the collective HAF to which we have all been exposed, even if we have never read even one Horatio Alger novel, can make us feel both frustrated and guilty about our lack of accomplishment.

It's all very fine to say that in a democracy such as ours, anyone can become president of anything; but the statistical chances of that happening are about one in ten million. And if we don't make it, we're not failures or somehow lacking in gumption, grit, or any of those other qualities that football coaches and managers of sales organizations prize so highly.

There are indeed some instances when daydreams can be bad for us, both individually and collectively. If you are having any of the following problems, you should probably rethink your approach to fantasy, and you may even need some professional help:

1. Anyone who has a persistent fantasy involving violence, blood, and hurting other people has a problem. If you have any repeated daydream that you yourself consider bizarre, even if it sounds OK to others, you might want to talk this over with a professional. We all have some odd or extremely fanciful daydreams, but most of our daydreams are at least moderately tied to our daily realities. It's the recurrence, indeed *domination* of all thought by a single violent or bizarre theme that signals a problem.

2. If your daydreams become more real than real life, and if, like Susan, you can't concentrate on your daily tasks because your fantasy world is so much more pleasant, you also probably have a problem. This is one that you can usually solve on

160 your own by simply rationing your daydreaming

times, preferably concentrating them during your leisure hours.

3. If your goals consistently are higher than your ability to reach (like Maximilian), and this makes you feel guilty, frustrated, or disappointed, you also may need help in separating fantasy from reality. This is especially true if your inability to reach your daydream goal immobilizes you so that you accomplish less than you might if you lowered your expectations of yourself.

4. If you find yourself accepting a fairy tale (be it Cinderella, Horatio Alger, or the story about George Washington and the cherry tree) as a pattern for your own or anyone else's life, the time has come for you to separate myth from fact. In a way, our collective fantasies can be much more dangerous than our individual ones. Fantasies about leaders, when shared by millions of citizens, can lead nations into self-destructive courses of action. The French and Germans might have maintained their newly won empires had they not invaded the vast, cold regions of Russia. We in the United States might be much better off had we not shared the fantasies of Kennedy, Johnson, and Nixon that U.S. ground and air forces could serve as the "policemen" of Southeast Asia. Such shared fantasies can lead to political, social, and economic disasters, as well as personal ones—but that is not what this book is about.

Fantasies
that Prevent Boredom
and Help
with Decision Making

Many of our days and weeks move along with very little to change them or to make them interesting. After a while, we may ask ourselves: "Is this all there is to life? Am I missing the excitement and variety that others seem to experience? What can I do to bring something new and stimulating into this routine?" Often there is not very much you can do to change your life patterns: office procedures must be followed, notes typed up, beds made, meals cooked; whatever your role, you usually have a steady scenario that you must follow unless you wish to court disaster, including the loss of your job and/or spouse.

Gauguin may have been able to escape the daily grind of a secure job in a French bank by giving up family life to devote himself solely to painting. Despite the romantic legends about him, he might eventually have lived to regret his decision to settle in the South Seas, for he continued while painting his masterpieces to yearn for mail from his family members who lived in Denmark. Since then, others have tried similar routes. Recently, a well-known, well-paid writer for one of the largest-circulation magazines decided to throw over his job and family to take off for Pago Pago. He wrote all about it in *New York* magazine. His first article was full of enthusiasm and hope; he'd really made his fantasy come true. A later article sounded discouraged and disillusioned. Tropical islands are not what they are cracked up to be, he had decided. They lack such elementary comforts as good sanitation and a decent, varied food supply. And, unless one wishes to spend every evening watching the palm trees swaying in the breeze, there's little else going on by way of entertainment. The native maidens turned out to be overweight and unimpressed with a middle-aged American, the island had no TV reception, and the only nearby movie house played old Tarzan films once a month. He spent his evenings watching the palm trees swaying in the breeze, and apparently decided after six months that if you've seen one swaying palm tree, you've seen them all. When last heard from he was back in civilization (Westport, Connecticut, if we remember correctly), looking for a job and thinking of getting married again.

Most of us are either too sensible or too cowardly to walk out on the life we know into one about which we know nothing. But, without damage to ourselves, our families, or our earning power, we can certainly wander off anywhere at anytime in our heads. We can also use everyday occurrences to create fascinating stories. What about that tall, bald man we see every day on our way to work? What's in the bulging briefcase he carries? Government secrets, or a stash of cocaine, or just his ham sandwich? And what about that nattily dressed gentleman who seems to spend so much time at the railroad station, looking in the mirror over the chewing gum machine? He may be a poor orphan boy who fought his way up from a lonely childhood to success in the haberdashery business, or perhaps he's a minor member of the Godfather's family, carrying policy slips to a drop-off point. Or what about that attractive young woman we see regularly at the drugstore counter?

165

Is she the mistress of a well-known financier who keeps her in style in a fancy downtown apartment, even though, for some unknown reason, he finds it necessary to meet her at the drugstore? Or is she a bright young physician who is thinking over the brain surgery she will be performing that afternoon, to the admiration and amazement of all her male colleagues?

In your imagination you may follow any of these people through endless scenarios. As you are sitting on a bus, each face in the crowd can become a story in itself. If you find that your fantasies are becoming routine, right along with the rest of your life, you can change a small detail in your daily routine. You might take a different route to work, or start to shop for groceries at a new store—and thereby meet a whole new cast of characters. Or you might strike up a simple conversation with a stranger sitting next to you. Sometimes a phrase like "Hot enough for you?" or "Fine weather for ducks" (in a rainstorm) may get a simple conversation going. Obviously, you're not going to learn a whole lot about the stranger, and he or she won't know any more about you. The idea of starting the conversation is not to acquire a new lifetime friend, but to get responses on which you can build, in your mind, a whole new fantasy picture about the person.

DAILY DECISIONS

On the other hand, there are days when you wish that life would turn out to be a little *more* monotonous. You've got an important decision to make, and it worries you. Should you ask your boss for a raise and threaten to quit if he won't consider it? Should you allow your teenage son to buy a motorbike? Should you tell your husband that you need time off from the daily grind and would like to spend three evenings a week taking a college extension course in Medieval and Renaissance Art History?

166 Or there may be more long-term and complex

decisions which you may want to take a week or even a month to mull over. Do you want to accept that promotion which will require you to move to a new and strange community? Do you want to switch careers altogether? Do you want to break off a love affair which seems to be going nowhere so that you can make a new start? Do you want to ask your wife/husband for a separation? Simple or complex, seemingly unimportant or critical, you can use your imagination and fantasy to help you in all kinds of problem situations.

Actually, all of us do some of this without realizing it or without planning it methodically. How often have we mentally redecorated the living room, sometimes with antiques, sometimes in French Provincial, and sometimes in Danish Modern, before we start actually making the rounds of furniture stores to begin the project? How often have we had imaginary conversations with employers, lovers, friends, and enemies getting whatever was bothering us off our chests? The difference between this kind of free-floating fantasy and the kind that you might use to solve a specific problem is one of planning and control. You'll be using your imagination not just to pass the time (as you did when you became bored with your daily routine), but systematically with a specific result in mind.

Let's take a simple problem first. A young woman, whom we shall call Jane, works as a research assistant on a small trade magazine dealing with the hardware industry. Jane's main task is to do background research to check out factual material in various articles that have been submitted for publication by outside writers. Most of her work deals with complicated, technical details and she has to keep her wits about her in order not to make mistakes. ("Three mistakes and you're fired," her boss told her when she first applied for the job.)

She shares her small office with another young woman, who has some unpleasant and distracting

167

habits but who is otherwise a perfectly agreeable person. Her office companion is a proofreader who has to review printed galleys for mistakes in spelling, punctuation, etc. She has a tendency to read the material to herself in an audible whisper. When she isn't doing that, she's humming the same tune from a now defunct Broadway musical over and over again. On top of that, she rubs her feet across the floor, making unpleasant squeaking noises. All of this is so disconcerting to poor Jane that she has difficulty concentrating on her own, not too interesting job. So she wonders what she should do before she makes those three disastrous mistakes and gets fired.

The situation is becoming so disturbing that she thinks about it all the time. It's keeping her from going to sleep at night. As she rides to work on the bus every morning, she thinks again and again about all the annoyance her office mate's behavior is causing her. She feels sure that her blood pressure must be rising.

Jane has considered telling the other woman that she's being driven up a wall—in a tactful way, of course, because she knows that they will continue to share working space unless, or until, one of them quits or gets fired. And as far as she knows, the other woman needs her job as much as Jane needs hers. But the situation has become so emotional for her that she fears she might lose her temper and create a scene if she lets her office partner know what's bothering her. She could use her imagination to defuse her anger, and one way to do this is through laughter.

She might begin with some really wild possibilities. The tunes her office partner is humming are really a code to some spies in the next room; the FBI has found out and is storming into the office to take her noisy roommate off to jail; the other woman has been captured by savages in the jungle and is still humming and whispering to herself about hardware articles while being lowered

168 into a cooking pot; her office partner leans over

backwards too far and tips her chair. She lands on the floor still humming away. If the fantasy is funny enough, it will probably clear up some of the anger.

After she has defused her anger, Jane can use her imagination to deal with the practical problems at hand. Now that she's cooled down, should she bring up the subject with the hummer herself? Jane can go through several imaginary conversations, trying everything from plain English to circuitous tact. She can also imagine the answers the other woman will probably give, having worked with her for some time.

If she comes to the conclusion, through these imaginary conversations, that the direct approach will just cause more trouble, she may decide to talk it over with the boss. Here again, she can use her fantasy to gauge what results such a talk would have. What are some of the outside possibilities? Perhaps the boss is having an affair with the proof-reader. In that case, he'd resent Jane's complaints. But all she has to do is picture the two characters in bed together to come to the inevitable conclusion that this particular scenario is about as ridiculous as the one about the savages and the cooking pot. Let's say the boss says something like this: "Look, Jane, I can see you've got a problem...but we just don't have another office space for either one of you, so you'll have to make the best of it." What then? Well, perhaps there is another way of arranging the desk so that the noise will not be so audible. Jane, in her mind, can rearrange the furniture. After she has done that for a while, she comes up with a real-life solution: by putting her desk next to the window with its humming airconditioner, she won't be disturbed by that old Broadway song any longer. The airconditioner will drown out her roommate's voice. And that particular sound will not distract her. Hallelujah, she's got a solution, worked out entirely in her mind which she will apply in real life!

Here's another way of using your imagination **169**

to deal with a simple everyday problem: try to imagine you are a person whom you especially admire—a movie star, a bright, assertive friend, your older brother or sister, for instance. Really throw yourself into the personality of that role model. Try to think the way he or she thinks, and talk the way he or she talks. You might even want to try emulating your model's speech patterns, walk, and mannerisms in front of a mirror. You'll obviously do this when you are unobserved, or else a bystander might think you've lost your mind. Then try to act, first in your fantasy, and then in real life, the way you think your role model would act in a similar situation. It often works.

Let's take the case of Steve, the owner of a small suburban home with an immaculate front yard. He lives next to Hank, a born slob. Hank puts his trash can out front, usually a day before the collector is scheduled to arrive, and the wind blows papers, potato peelings, and other undesirable articles all over Steve's prize lawn. Steve has some problems asserting himself. He gets madder and madder about the mess in front of his house but can't bring himself to confront Hank with the situation. Here's a fantasy that has helped a great many unassertive people like Steve make their point with relatively little discomfort:

Steve can imagine himself to be another person, one whom he really admires for his courage and consistency. Let's say Steve is a Spencer Tracy or Humphrey Bogart fan. He can then picture himself as Tracy or Bogart looking out the door and finding the daily collection of trash in his shrubbery. In his new, more glamorous and daring character, he can picture himself going to see Hank and saying, in a friendly but firm fashion: "Look fellow, I realize you've got a lot of garbage, and you obviously can't keep it around the house, but please get a bigger garbage can, or one with a tighter lid, and wait until the day the trash is collected. As you can see, although you may not have noticed, **170** my front yard is getting pretty trashy looking."

If the imaginary Hank gives Steve (transformed mentally into Bogart or Tracy) a rough time, he can talk back to his neighbor, using the kind of language and demeanor his heroes might have used. After Steve has practiced that for a while, he will probably be able to talk things over with Hank in real life. Although Hank sees him only as good, old Steve, the friendly compliant neighbor, Steve can be acting out his hero character. He will probably surprise Hank with his confidence and assertiveness, and something will get done about the front yard mess. Also, Steve may be able to use a similar technique in dealing with his obnoxious, interfering sister-in-law or that co-worker who is always staying out two hours for lunch and asking Steve to cover for him at the office.

One woman put this technique to work in a very different situation. Olivia had been divorced for about five years. Her last child had recently left home for college and she felt very lonely. She left her house in the country and moved to an apartment hotel in a nearby city where she knew few people. Since she did not feel much like cooking a whole meal for herself alone, she often ate in the hotel dining room, at a small table in a corner. Soon she discovered that a pleasant-looking man, about her age, regularly had his meals at a nearby table. He, also, was always alone. She felt intrigued and somewhat attracted and longed to talk to him. But she was very shy and found herself unable to start a conversation. It was obvious to her that he too was shy, although she noticed that he glanced in her direction frequently.

One evening Olivia remembered that her friend Ruth, a lively woman a few years younger than herself, frequently told of meeting attractive and eligible men in hotel dining rooms, on board cruise ships, or even sitting next to her on the commuter train to work. She began to think of what Ruth would do in a situation similar to hers. Would she just quietly pass by the man on the way to her table? She would not. She'd probably drop a

171

casual remark to the stranger, something like: "Nice weather isn't it?" or "That creamed chicken you are having looks really great, would you recommend it?" If that evoked only a polite, noncommittal answer, Ruth might say something like this the next time: "I notice you eat here quite often. Do you live in this hotel?" Olivia could even imagine Ruth saying: "Do you mind if I join you for a while? I've noticed that you've been alone every day as I have, and sometimes I feel like talking to someone over dinner." She can then picture the man breaking into a broad smile and saying something like this: "Gee, I've been trying to get up enough courage to talk to you without having you think I was attempting a pickup. Please sit down, by all means." From then on, she could fantasize about the relationship between Ruth and the stranger growing and blossoming, ending perhaps with a honeymoon on a cruise ship to the Caribbean.

After going through these fantasy conversations for a while, shy Olivia finally could bring herself (pretending to be Ruth) to say "good evening" to the stranger. The next night, he said "good evening" to her. They started to talk about the weather, the service at the hotel, the best dishes in the restaurant, and eventually the man came over to her table and *he* asked if he could join *her*. Both discovered that they had a great many tastes and interests in common. They are not off on a honeymoon trip to the islands or anywhere else, but they often attend concerts, movies, and art shows together, and recently they took a weekend trip to the country. Olivia is much less lonely—and she's delighted that, by borrowing her friend's personality for a while, she met a new and interesting male companion.

Jane, Steve, and Olivia were able to use their fantasizing abilities to overcome the kinds of anxieties and shyness most of us experience. All three were caught in a vicious circle of negative feelings: frustration and anger in the case of Jane and Steve, loneliness and shyness in Olivia's case. But actually, all three faced some fairly simple options. There are times in all our lives when we are faced with *major* decisions with a variety of options open to us.

All of us, at some time, have to decide whether or not we want to terminate a long-standing relationship, move to another community, make a major career change, and other matters which may determine the future course of our lives. The techniques used in making simple, less important decisions can also work for us when we are contemplating much more important questions. Two social scientists, Dr. Irving L. Janis and Dr. Leon Mann, have recently published an important book called *Decision Making*. On looking over all of the past literature on the decision-making process, the two authors came to the conclusion that in order to arrive at the best possible solution to problems, would-be decision-makers should engage in a systematic program of "vigilant information gathering." This would obviously involve gathering all possible relevant facts, both positive and negative, before making up one's mind. But are facts always enough? Since most of us are uncomfortable with chance, would the possession of volumes of statistical and other hard data persuade us to make a rational decision whose consequences we may fear?

One way to get around this dilemma is to get accustomed to the possible consequences, by playing them over in your mind again and again, in a variety of ways, before attempting to take significant action.

Let's assume that the problem you are tackling is a change in jobs. This is a major step which might bring about a great improvement in your life. It could also lead to an even greater disaster. In weighing all the possible consequences, you might do better by working through your worst fears first. A thoroughly negative scenario is usually a good start in such cases. What is the worst that can happen if you decide to quit your present, **173**

secure but dull job, to take up that new and chal-
lenging one? You might hate the job; the new employer might hate you; you might get fired after a
few weeks and have to look for a new position.
Meanwhile, you'll be pretty thoroughly strapped
financially.

It's not much fun to play such a scenario in
your mind, but it's still helpful for making valid
judgments. You can imagine yourself arriving at
the office the first day and finding that the work is
not what you had supposed. You can play a scene
casting your new boss as a demanding, short-
tempered Simon Legree. You can picture the red
dismissal slip in your pay envelope, and the con-
sequent drain on your slender bank account. If
you want to carry this further, you can picture
yourself opening late notices from the landlord,
liquor dealer, favorite department store, and several
utility companies. After you've played these de-
pressing scenes in your head, you can ask yourself
whether you are risking this kind of trouble in real
life. You have met the employer. Is he really the
ogre you've made him out to be in your mind? Is it
really possible that the work will be so difficult
and boring? Are those fears of finding the dismissal
notice clipped to your pay check realistic? Would
you actually find it so difficult to get a new job? Is
your bank account as low as it seems in your worst
nightmares? Is there no way you could manage,
even if you were to find yourself unemployed for a
time? What about unemployment compensation,
for instance? Often, by playing out our worst fears,
we can look at them in context. We can alleviate or
dismiss much anticipatory anxiety in this way.

On the other hand, what is the worst that
could happen if you don't take that new job? In
your mind, sit down at your old desk and really feel
the boredom that often attacks you during your
working day. Imagine yourself ten years later still
at that same desk with the same dull, unchallenging
work.

Then compare the fear of insecurity in your

new job with the lack of interest and excitement in your present position. Which makes you feel worse?

Now you can play both job situations over quite differently: letting your highest hopes and expectations take over. The new employer turns out to be more intelligent, fascinating, and appreciative of your abilities than he did during that first interview. After a few weeks, there's a meeting of everyone in your department, and your contribution is praised to the skies. You get a raise and a promotion, and from there on it's up all the way. Then put your present job in this kind of perspective. Your job routine is changed so that you have an excellent opportunity to prove your as yet unappreciated talents. All those who have taken you for granted suddenly realize that they have an undiscovered future vice-president in their midst. Which of these two scenarios makes you feel better? Of course, both the negative and positive fantasies about either of the two jobs are unrealistic in the extreme, so now you mix the two. Play through, in your imagination, what you can realistically expect if you decide to take either course. Mix your fears and anxieties with your hopes and expectations. If you can do this, you will probably be able much more confidently to use that "vigilant thought processing" Janis and Mann recommend, and you will feel freer and less anxious about coming to a final decision about which way to turn.

To sum up the few steps you can use to help you solve your day-to-day problems, from minor and annoying to major and life-changing:

1. Clear your mind temporarily of both fears and hopeful expectations. If all your feelings are flooding in on you at once, they tend to get confusing. You may even panic and become incapable of any decision. Relax. Do the exercises in Chapter 5.

2. Most of the relatively simple problems that we find difficult to deal with have already caused us some frustration and anger. Use humorous fantasies to lighten up the situation. Then imagine yourself

175

tackling the difficulty at hand. Try several solutions in your mind. Work out a number of imaginary conversations you might have with others involved in the problem. You may just hit on a solution that will work in real life. If not, you'll probably at least overcome your hesitation and start acting instead of worrying.

3. If you have always considered yourself a 90-pound weakling, emotionally speaking, pretend that you are one of your favorite heroes or heroines: Spencer Tracy, Humphrey Bogart, Katharine Hepburn, or the Bionic Woman. If you have a more realistic frame of mind, try one of your most admired friends or relatives. Devise a mental scenario in which he or she solves the difficulty while you are in the personality of your admired hero or heroine. Then try solving it in real life, calling on the heroic qualities you've imagined.

4. When you have to make a major decision, find out all the facts first, of course. Then, in order to use those facts to their best advantage, devise a number of scenarios in which you play through the consequences of your decision. Start with the worst consequences, thus allowing yourself to feel vicariously all the insecurity and anxiety you might feel. Then take the most optimistic course. Eventually, try mixing both positive and negative effects, until you've arrived at a scenario that seems most realistic to you. Once you've reached that state, start applying those facts you have gathered.

Your imaginative life gives you tremendous power over the future if you know how to exercise fantasy systematically, allowing your free flights of imagination to anticipate the worst and the happiest possibilities, and then gradually zeroing in on what is realistically possible in your particular situation.

Using Mind Rehearsals to Improve Your Skill at Sports and Games

Any physical or mental skill requires practice. Few people realize that such practice does not have to take place only while they are actually performing on a playing field or in a gymnasium; one can practice almost any skill when one is alone and is able to let one's mind wander: sitting in the living room after dinner, riding on a plane or bus or train, or walking in the woods. During these quiet times, the mind can go through a whole series of exercises that might prepare the body for more effective functioning. In the past, people have tended to view daydreaming and fantasy as cutting down on one's best physical functioning. Athletes were supposed to be down-to-earth, prosaic individuals who spent their free time sleeping, eating, and watching other athletes, Westerns, and police shows on television. Today, coaches are actually teaching their teams to use their fantasies to attain better performances. Several coaches have actually employed psychologists to teach their athletes how to use their fantasies to better their physical performances.

Philosophers and theoreticians about human action have long recognized that our mental capacities provide us with a means of engaging in movements or conversations before they actually occur overtly. Freud referred to thought as "experimental action" in which one can try out behaviors with a minimum of risk or expenditure of energy. There are hundreds of situations in our lives in which we anticipate dancing, playing in a game or contest, undertaking a complicated rock climb. All require complex physical movements, but when we are in bed at night, when we are sitting at our desk in school or the office, we are prevented from engaging in real physical practice. Will mental rehearsal make a difference?

The idea of being able to perform a skill physically which we have practiced previously in our mind appears not only in philosophical and rather complicated essays on sports, but also, on a much more simple level, on television, in novels, and in films. One example is the film *The Music Man* (which tends to reappear every July 4 on network TV). The hero of this musical is a flimflam artist and traveling salesman who persuades the people in the towns he visits to buy instruments and uniforms for a boys' band he promises to organize. He convinces everybody that he can teach the youngsters how to play by using a unique system he has developed. In actuality, he doesn't know one note from another, but he persuades parents and children alike that if they just *think* hard enough about playing the tuba, they will be able to play the tuba, as soon as the instruments the school board has ordered arrive. The day before the shipment comes in, he quietly leaves town, and the citizens of the town, once they find out they have been ripped off, can't even ride him out on a rail. But in one Indiana town the music master finds true love and sees the light. After the instruments arrive, he stays, ready to take his punishment at the hands of the outraged citizenry. But, lo and behold, his technique has worked! The band which has only practiced on nonexistent tubas, trumpets, and trombones plays magnificently as soon as the boys **179** get their equipment. Everybody marches around town playing on the band instruments and singing that great marching tune, "Seventy-Six Trombones," loudly and with gusto. It's a great ending for a movie. In real life, it's for the birds.

Mental practice can be valuable, but only once you've already learned the basic physical skills. A psychologist studied a group of children who were learning to jump rope. Once they'd all learned the basics he divided them into three groups. One group continued regular rope-jumping practice. A second group practiced only in *imagination,* going through the steps and movements mentally again and again. The third group did other things unrelated to rope-jumping practice. When tested later the children who practiced physically did best of all, but those who practiced *mentally* were not too far behind and they far surpassed the third group.

Of course, we are not trying to suggest that you will be able to substitute mental practice completely for physical practice. But some of the best athletes have told of using fantasy at appropriate times as part of their overall preparation for effective play.

Football player O. J. Simpson told a *Playboy* magazine interviewer that some of his best plays had been practiced in his mind long before he executed them on the field. When praised for a particularly spectacular feat that he apparently had achieved for the first time, he said: "I've run that play so many times in my mind, I just *knew* it. All the runs I have made a million times in my mind. Cats come up to me afterwards and say: 'How'd you know to do that...?' I tell them, 'Hey, I'm in my car driving down the San Diego freeway or a freeway somewhere else, and I'm always running all kinds of plays in my mind.' I picture a play over ground I've never run before. I don't have to be in a room watching films to know what the other guy is going to be doing... what moves to put on him."

180 The system seems to work for Mr. Simpson,

although we would not actually recommend daydreaming about football, or anything else for that
matter, while driving on a California freeway.

In an article in *Psychology Today* (July
1976), psychologist Richard M. Suinn discussed
the reactions of some of the athletes he has met
and helped to train. For instance, Paul Pesthy, who
has participated as a Pentathlon contender in several Olympic games, reports that he uses the time
between matches to reduce the tension of the last
match. Unlike O. J. Simpson, he does not use his
fantasy to plan his next encounter. Instead, he
does something completely unrelated: he puts a
towel over his head, closes his eyes, and imagines
that he is drawing circles within circles on the
ground.

On the other hand, imagery definitely related
to the sport was tried with the ski team at Colorado State University. Dr. Suinn attempted to
teach the team members a system of progressive
relaxation (similar to the methods described in
Chapter 5), combined with what he calls "imagery
rehearsal." He also calls this system "visuomotor
behavior rehearsal" or VMBR, for short. "The
method can be divided into three simple steps," he
says, "relaxation, the practice of imagery, and the
use of imagery for strengthening psychological or
motor skills."

For the Colorado ski team the system seems
to have worked very well. They cut down on skiing
errors by mentally repeating the correct actions,
and they became more aggressive than the control
group which was not given similar imagery training.

Images are apparently also employed by skiers
who have not had formal training. They, like O. J.
Simpson, simply arrived at the system themselves.
Jean-Claude Killy, a three-time winner of Olympic
Gold Medals in skiing, reported that, because of an
injury, his only preparation for a particular race
was to ski it mentally. He also reported that that
race turned out to be one of his best.

Many psychologists have come to the conclu-   **181**

sion that a successful performance is one which involves an almost automatic response which is so completely natural and spontaneous that one is not even aware of what is happening until, in retrospect, one realizes that one has given an almost flawless performance. Psychologist Mihalyi Csikszentmihalyi has written of such activities, which he calls "flow experiences," in his book *Boredom and Anxiety*. He defines "flow" as an experience of complete unity with the activity in which one is involved. Among the people studied for "flow" were rock climbers, surgeons, and others who have combined the optimal relationship of challenge with actual competence. When challenge and competence met, his subjects found themselves completely one with the rocks they were climbing or the patient on whom they were operating. In retrospect, many of these subjects could not quite figure out why they had experienced "flow" during a particular activity. But most indicated that they often went through extensive mental practice sessions before actually going ahead with their task.

A gymnast described a similar experience to one of the co-authors. He reported that there was one exercise on the parallel bars he could not seem to master. When he got up to do this exercise, he would almost always fail. Eventually, he started doing it in his head, slowly, step by step. Then he tried it again physically. He found that the mental practice had made it possible for him to perform the exercise flawlessly.

The impression was confirmed by a psychologist, Dr. Allen Richardson, who has worked extensively with gymnasts. He asked one group of these athletes to practice all their skills very carefully, but he did not give them any additional imagery training. Another group was trained to perform the exercises mentally as well as physically. The second group did substantially better in competition.

Quite recently psychologists Michael Mahoney and Marshall Avener of Pennsylvania State University studied a group of American gymnasts preparing for the Olympics. These athletes filled out questionnaires about their mental and physical attitudes and behavior patterns before the actual Olympic tryouts. After the trials, when everyone's scores were known, their questionnaire responses were compared to their performance ratings by the judges. Those athletes who performed best reported that they were much more likely to practice mentally and to dream about successful performances. It is interesting to note that while they were nervous *before* the competition and did a lot of mental rehearsal, once they actually were in the situation performing they were less likely to be thinking about a current move than the less successful gymnasts. The prior mental rehearsal and dreaming permitted them to move directly into a "flow" state in which they seemed to become effortlessly "one" with the activity.

Dr. Timothy Gallwey's work on *The Inner Game of Tennis* implies a similar approach. Thinking about the game, fantasizing moves and countermoves, and mentally replaying our strokes can help us detect mistakes or awkward or self-defeating moves. But once in the game itself fantasy is disastrous. The pregame fantasies should lead to a complete concentration on the game.

Ballet dancers and musicians go through a similar process. They feel that their mental training deepens the emotional quality they convey, because they feel so much surer of themselves and they are freer to concentrate totally on their performances. The mind can usually run just a bit ahead of where the body is. You can often stretch a little further or move a little faster in your mind than with your body. But that adds to the excitement.

There should be one caveat, though. As Gallwey suggests, while you are actually engaged in the activity, you can't let your mind wander on fantasies.

If you are playing another game in your mind than the one in which you are actually engaged 183 with your body, you'll find that the ball is whizzing over your head. If you are looking at a picture in your mind's eye, you are not looking at the ball. Some sports figures have reported that becoming engaged in daydreams *while out on the playing field* has hurt their performance. Here are some quotes from the experiences of some of our finest tennis players, for instance, as John McPhee wrote in "The Levels of the Game" for *New Yorker* magazine:

> *The mind of Arthur Ashe is wandering. It wanders sometimes in crucial moments...such as now...in the second set of semi-finals of the first United States Open Championship at Forest Hills....With the premium now maximum on every shot, Ashe is nonetheless thinking of what he considers the ideal dinner: fried chicken, rice and baked beans. During matches the ideal dinner is sometimes uppermost in Ashe's mind. Graebner, like other tennis players, knows this and counts on it. "He'll always daydream. That's one of his big hang-ups. That's why he escapes to the movies so much. But in a match he won't dream long enough. I wish he would do it longer."*

A top-notch woman player, Chris Evert Lloyd, has reported a similar experience following her loss in the semi-finals of an international tournament to Billie Jean King, who had come from behind to defeat her. Ms. Lloyd told a *New York Times* reporter why she had lost the game after taking a very strong initial lead: "I started thinking about what I was going to do after I had won," she confessed.

This is the kind of daydreaming that has given fantasy a bad name in the sports world.

Interestingly enough, the fantasy and mind image system works for games in which mental, not physical skills, are important. Chess players, for instance, have to picture their partners' moves

184

and their own several turns ahead. Bridge players have to try to discern from the bidding what cards their partners and opponents might be holding. In these activities, the use of mind images and fantasy is so obvious that it is rarely thought of or mentioned.

Here are some specific steps you might try if you want to improve your performance at an athletic skill or game:

1. Do the actual physical exercises slowly and carefully. Then relax and visualize your performance in as much detail as you can recall. Imagine that you are actually in the situation, using all your other senses as well as sight. You can feel, smell, and taste what is happening. Run the images through your mind over and over again. If you stumbled at one point, replay the mistake and try to discover where you went wrong. If you have been particularly successful in another instance, play it over and try to discover what you did right.

2. In your mind, put yourself in a competitive situation. Let's say your game is tennis. Plan your strategy, and try to picture your opponent's counter-strategy. Again, make your mind pictures as vivid as possible. Imagine your muscles stretching for a jump, or the feeling of tension when you are not sure you can return the ball. Once you have allowed the experience to develop as vividly as possible, keep practicing it during the day whenever you have a free moment. (O. J. Simpson notwithstanding, avoid this kind of activity when you are driving a car or operating a machine.) Imagination, incidentally, is also a skill. Just as you will become more effective in a sport when you practice, you'll also be able to produce better mind pictures as you keep experimenting with them.

3. If you want to psyche out your opponent, you will have to develop some intuitive powers. Intuition is not just inborn in a few lucky females; probably anyone (males included) can acquire it by using powers of observation and imagination con-

185

sistently. Through intuition, you will probably be able to predict whatever countermoves your opponent is likely to make.

Studies of chess players have shown that champions do not necessarily have a better capacity to visualize the board than mediocre players. They don't necessarily have better memories either. But the better players have practiced, in actuality and in their minds, hundreds of moves and countermoves over and over again. They have tried every position and almost every possibility. When they are actually confronted with a problem during a match, they can quickly sense what's happening, and respond with a countermove almost instinctively. The champion players sense where their own moves and their opponents' moves fit into some kind of broader pattern which they have thoroughly explored in their minds. Often, these players quickly make the right move apparently without thought. They can't explain why they were able to do this, but to an observer the reason is clear: they are following a scheme they have observed over and over again in their minds.

Those who are able to do this are most likely to have the "flow" experience. They will not only be more successful than if they had not practiced, they will also feel happier, more relaxed, and more at ease with themselves as they find they are able to accomplish top performance naturally and without any apparent hesitation or strain.

4. After you have discovered, by repeating your past performances where you have made mistakes, don't replay the mistakes. It's only too easy to wish that you could change what you've done in the past. You can't. You can only learn from it for the future. So, in your mind, eliminate the mistake and play the set or the game differently. One of the best features of mind imagery is that you can at least change the past in your head—and the future as well. You will be able to improve your skills by recognizing a mistake and then proceeding to work the situation out more effectively. You

won't be able to do this if you go through constant binges of self-recrimination. Telling yourself that you should have done something differently is self-defeating. Do it differently in your mind, and then proceed to the present and the future.

5. Don't set impossible goals for yourself. It is probably safe to set your standards a little higher than what you might be expected to achieve. But if your performance is constantly far below your expectations, you'll eventually become discouraged and quit. If you are just learning to ski and you would like to imagine yourself as Jean-Claude Killy, it can't hurt, as long as you don't expect to have your daydream translated into reality through some form of magic. If you want to use fantasy to improve your performance (rather than to entertain yourself—a perfectly legitimate goal, if that's what you are really doing), you will have to stay fairly close to reality.

Stimulating
Imagination
in Your Children

C. R. Milne and Alice Liddell were very lucky children. Early in their lives, an imaginative and loving adult helped them create a whole imaginary world, including some very special fantasy companions who could get them through boring, lonely, and otherwise unhappy hours.

Christopher Robin Milne was an only child, and his father, writer A. A. Milne, worried that his son might miss out on the companionship that children in larger families enjoy. So he created for his child a playmate, Winnie the Pooh, the teddy bear friend who lived "behind a green door in another part of the forest." Other children might invent imaginary companions for themselves, but few are lucky enough to have a writer-father who can create such an amusing, lovable, and constantly entertaining one as Pooh.

As a small girl, Alice Liddell made friends with a distinguished mathematician, Charles Lutwidge Dodgson, who served as a lecturer at Christ College, Oxford. Dodgson, possibly in order to disengage his mind from all those mathematical calculations, began telling Alice, the daughter of the college dean, fanciful and delightfully absurd stories in which he placed her into an imaginary world with all kinds of fascinating imaginary play-mates. Later, he decided to write down those stories, and they were published under his pseudonym: Lewis Carroll. The book, *Alice in Wonderland,* became an immediate success with adults as well as children. The stories even enchanted Queen Victoria, well-known for her disdainful put-down: "We are not amused."

You don't need to be a talented writer to help your children develop their imaginations. Many parents, however, aren't quite sure that fantasy and daydreaming are good for their youngsters. Some parents are even worried when they spot such tendencies in their children.

Betty and Jim Allen, for instance, brought their 5-year-old son, Jim Jr., to a child guidance clinic because he spent some of his time playing with an imaginary Labrador retriever called Rover. Betty was allergic to dog hair, so it was impossible for the Allens to keep a real dog around the premises. Rover was apparently Jim Jr.'s answer to his unrealized yearning for a pet. The Allens were not so much concerned about their youngster's present fantasy life, but they had visions of Jim Jr. taking Rover along to college, and, God forbid, to work. They had seen the movie *Harvey* on television and felt that if Elwood P. Dowd could take his six-foot rabbit into a bar, their son might be tempted, 20 years from now, to take Rover into a law court. (They hoped their son would be a lawyer like his father.)

The social worker at the child guidance clinic assured them that Jim Jr. was an entirely normal child who knew that Rover was a figment of his imagination, and who would almost certainly give up his play with the make-believe dog by the time he was in the first or second grade. She also explained that children know the difference between reality and fantasy, even if it may seem to the parents that the youngster's imaginary world is **191** exceedingly real and concrete. Underneath it all, Jim Jr. is completely aware that Rover is an imaginary dog, even though he tells his mother to be on the lookout, when shopping at the supermarket, for the latest pet food for the animal.

Actually, all children engage in some kind of make-believe play. It's a natural part of their intellectual, social, and emotional growth process. Taking different roles, talking to themselves while pretending that someone else is in the room to listen, making a block look like a car or a piece of paper like an airplane—that's all part of a child's development. It's a way that children incorporate the complex material they find all around into their own still-limited range of ideas. Therefore, it's not a waste of time; children's imaginative play is an important learning experience which parents should encourage. If they don't, the youngster will eventually give up this kind of activity. Young children have an amazing knack of guessing what their parents do and do not approve of—even if the parents don't verbally express their preferences. We have discovered through extensive research that an imaginative, playful child is usually a happier, better adjusted one than his or her less imaginative companions. This is due to a number of reasons.

First of all, make-believe play is fun. In all of our research, we have found that children who play a lot of make-believe games seem to be just plain happier than those who are not involved in pretend play. Researchers watching such fantasy-play children tend to rate them as showing more signs of happiness; they smile more and seemingly are filled with what social scientists call "positive emotions."

Second, as we have said previously, all of us would be better off as adults if we had a well-developed sense of imagery and fantasy. The time to start developing these skills, just like other skills, is in childhood.

Third, a child engaged in imaginative play is actually learning all kinds of cognitive skills. When
such children talk to themselves, they are actually

practicing combinations of new words they may have heard and do not quite understand. Researchers have considerable evidence that imagination in early childhood and a rich vocabulary tend to go together.

Fourth, a child is using imaginative play to practice coping with a variety of situations. Youngsters, in their games, try out various kinds of experiences, at least some of which they will have as they get older. For instance, youngsters who are not quite old enough to start school, but who are worried about beginning this kind of drastic new life, may play "class and teacher" with other children or with their dolls. Even playing "doctor" is a relatively harmless way of dealing with their often puzzling feelings about sexuality.

Sometimes in play situations they develop some real interests which will continue throughout their adult lives. Obviously, the parents of a youngster who plays fireman or policeman should not plan to register the child for early admission to the local police academy or firefighting school. But there are some young children who started acting out their life ambitions at a surprisingly early age.

For instance, one young woman who is now a law professor at an excellent university started playing lawyer, judge, and jury with her dolls, starting at about age 5. Her grandfather was a well-known and outstanding judge who often took the little girl to his office, and who told her about some of the fascinating things that happened in his court. The child would reenact these stories, interpreted in her own way, as play. By the time she was 10 years old, she had given up the doll jury and was reading biographies of Clarence Darrow. When she was 12, she wrote to the producer of the *Perry Mason* show, which she was seeing on its tenth rerun, telling about all the legal mistakes Perry was making in the courtroom. She received a letter of thanks, indicating that "other lawyers have also criticized the program." She was naturally thrilled beyond words to have been taken for a real lawyer.

193

A fifth benefit of make-believe games is that children who take on a variety of roles in this way become more sensitive to the emotions of other people. There's nothing like learning, early on, what it is like to walk in someone else's moccasins, to allow a youngster to understand that all Indians aren't villains or that cowboys are not always the good guys. Youngsters who are able to imagine themselves as someone else tend to become more tolerant of differences, more able to understand the ideas and feelings of others.

Sixth, children who have active imaginations and who are able to amuse themselves easily in almost any situation find it much easier to wait and delay when that is necessary. If you've ever sat in a pediatrician's or dentist's waiting room with a group of mothers and small children, this fact becomes very evident. Little Johnny is sitting on the floor, playing with a paper airplane his mother has made, smiling, laughing, and generally having a fine time. Three feet away, Joanie, whose mother is frantically trying to amuse her, is having a tantrum. She's just plain bored.

One of the co-authors recently observed a group of children on an airplane flight from the Orient. In 15 hours on the plane, some of the children spent a great deal of the time in highly imaginative play (much of it seemed to be concerned with space flights). Another group of children spent most of their time complaining and crying, driving themselves, the stewardesses (who kept bringing new play equipment), their parents, and the other passengers crazy.

This casual observation is borne out by research. One of the co-authors conducted a series of tests to discover whether children who had make-believe play as a resource were actually able to sit quietly and wait more comfortably than children who did not. Two groups of youngsters (one rated as highly imaginative, and the other as somewhat lacking in imagination) were asked to pretend that they were astronauts and that, as such, they would have to sit quietly in a chair while steering their spaceships through orbit. The imaginative children were able to do this for quite a long time; the less imaginative children got bored with the game very quickly. Even if there were not other advantages to helping our children improve their ability to play imaginatively, the fact that they are able to entertain themselves without driving their parents up the wall would be good enough reason for most harried mothers to encourage such an activity.

A seventh advantage of imagination is that children can learn actual problem-solving through play. Some of our imaginative teachers have known this fact for a long time and have taken advantage of this ability to keep youngsters fascinated with some of the usually duller aspects of learning. For instance, in some school systems, arithmetic is now taught through an imaginary market setup. The children sell token apples and oranges, furniture, and even cars for pretend money. They learn to add, subtract, divide, and multiply through this game (which adults would probably call "Monopoly") and they also learn to ask some of the right questions about the make-believe merchandise, thus becoming more knowledgeable consumers.

Finally, make-believe can serve as a useful alternative to aggression. It's much better to have little Timmy go "bang bang" at little Susie, whom he detests, than to have him bop her over the head with his sand shovel. It's also better for Timmy to throw a make-believe tantrum when, as Superman, he can't get his cape on, than to throw one in real life when his mother won't buy him a box of the sugar-heavy cereal he has seen advertised on TV. Make-believe tantrums can relieve all kinds of real-life frustration, and they end when the game is over. Real-life tantrums can be thrown in entirely inappropriate places and times, and they rarely end until Mom or Dad has dragged screaming Timmy off to the family car.

Lately there has been a great deal of worry about TV violence and concern as to whether the **195** vicarious experience of viewing this kind of blood-thirsty activity would tend to make a youngster more aggressive in real life. The answer to this question is not yet in; but there's a general feeling that a child who is already in some emotional trouble might well be adversely affected by a constant stream of violent TV images. However, that's entirely different from the kind of imaginary violence a child makes up to get over boredom, anger, or frustration. Children who spend more time playing Superman and crook, policeman and burglar, or animal tamer and lion, are less likely to be observed behaving with inappropriate aggression or physical violence toward playmates or parents.

How can a parent become playful enough to help a child develop those make-believe skills researchers have proven are so useful? Here are a few suggestions:

Try to recapture some of your own childhood experiences and fantasies.

Here's a good way to begin: Stretch out on a couch or on your bed, and imagine yourself as you were as a small child. You may even want to assume the position in which you used to lie in your crib when you were very young. Let your mind float backward in time. Fix on one event that took place as early in your life as possible and that you still remember vividly. Recall some of the specific settings of your early childhood. What was your bedroom like? Did it have curtains that blew in the wind on stormy nights and scared you so you hid under the blanket? Was the blanket scratchy or soft? Did the mattress have lumps? Did you have a tree house or a special hideaway in the attic? Try to recall some of the tastes and smells of your childhood as vividly as possible: your grandfather's pipe, your father's shaving tonic, the way the kitchen smelled just before Thanksgiving, the taste of Christmas cookies or of the stick ice cream your parents bought from the street vendor on hot days. Recall as much as you possibly can of the

196

positive and negative feelings of childhood. Actually, some therapists urge their adult patients to go through this experience of seeing and feeling themselves as small children again, but you are not doing this for any kind of therapy; you are doing it to help your children become more imaginative and to help you understand them better.

Watch your children carefully to see if you can interpret their feelings and reactions in the light of what you remember to have been your own.

Were you afraid of the dark, especially when the wind blew those curtains? You may find that you have ignored or rejected a child's similar fear because you felt that to encourage a youngster to tell, or to act out, his or her fright was a sign of weakness or overpermissiveness on your part. Now, remembering how you felt yourself, do you really want to send the child back into that dark, terrifying bedroom? Why not get a night light? At least, try to talk to him or her and to find out what, specifically, is so frightening.

Did turnips make you gag? If you remember clearly the aversion you had to one particular food which your parents insisted you had to eat, and which, as a result, still makes you feel sick, you might want to reconsider if you really want to force young Bobby to clean up his plate and eat all those carrots he hates.

Remember the year you were so afraid of your second grade teacher that you hid behind a snow bank for an hour before the school janitor found you? If young Amy tells you she's scared of a teacher, you will find it much easier to empathize with her, and you may be able to reassure her that Miss Sourdough really is not this year's candidate for the title of "Bad Witch of the East." She just looks a little angry occasionally, and for some people that's a natural expression. Besides, there'll be another teacher next term.

Remember how you liked to ride your bike **197**

down the long hill without holding on to the handlebars? It worried your mother just as much as it now worries you when Andy leaps down half a flight of stairs or Barbara climbs to the top of the maple tree in the yard. You still will want to warn the children not to do anything that is really dangerous, but you'll be able to understand their need for adventure and excitement a great deal better.

Once you have been able to place yourself closer to your children's world through your own imagination, you'll find that you not only understand their day-to-day joys and problems better, but are able to play with them and suggest games all of you will enjoy.

Trust your sense regarding the kinds of games and play for which your child is ready.
There has been a great deal of emphasis on so-called educational toys recently. The toy manufacturers seem to be telling us that if we start our youngsters on the right puzzle at age 2, they'll graduate from Harvard summa cum laude at age 20. Don't worry too much about getting the proper toys and books for a young child. What you and he or she can make up in your heads can be much more fun and much more educational than what comes between the covers of a book or out of a box. You may want to initiate some of the games you remember enjoying when you were your child's age. Or you may want to make up something entirely new. If you are having fun, so will the child.

Realize that even a very young child does not really want an adult as a full-fledged playmate.
Once you have the youngster started on his or her particular imaginary road, step tactfully out of the picture. If the child seems to be bogged down or starts becoming bored, you might want to step in again to suggest something new; but don't try to take over. If you do so consistently, the child will miss out on using his or her own imagination and fantasy while playing along with yours.

Remember that when children interact, they often let out some aggressive, hostile feelings through role-playing.

If your child and a playmate are shouting at each other while playing policeman and crook, teacher and naughty boy—hopefully, though, not Mommy and Daddy—allow them to do so. Step in only when the anger becomes real and physical and the weapons turn out to be blocks or baseball bats instead of words and/or imaginary guns or sticks. In that case, suggesting a slightly different and more peaceful game will usually save the situation.

If a child seems to have trouble getting started playing imaginative games, try to encourage him or her by making up simple stories or creating simple characters.

After you give the youngster this start, then let him or her continue the story, either verbally or in play form. There are some children who are not very verbal; they use their imaginations to draw or to model in clay, or to build skyscrapers or space-ships with their blocks or other building materials. Or they may want to act out situations or sing about them. Anything they want to do is fine—just as long as they don't hurt themselves or another child.

Understand that some highly imaginative children become very bothered by TV shows that don't bother adults at all.

Children can become almost as upset watching Donald Duck get lambasted by one of his enemies as they would be watching Starsky and Hutch being beaten bloody by a sadistic villain. Try to watch TV with your child and interpret any material that may be upsetting or otherwise over the child's head. The same, to a lesser degree, is probably true for books. The pre-radio, pre-TV generation grew up on some children's stories that were not exactly all gentle and sweet. Remember that witch in Hansel and Gretel who wanted to bake the children in her oven and eat them? Remember **199**

Snow White's stepmother, who sent the little girl out to be shot by a hunter? Or the little match girl who froze to death in the snow? Some of these and other stories are classics, and if your children enjoy them, they are probably fine. On the other hand, it's only natural for a particularly imaginative child to become upset by this kind of material. If he or she does, try to explain more about the story or choose some other kind of book, just as you would choose a less violent type of TV program.

Cooperating with children to stimulate them in developing their imaginative skills is one of the most rewarding experiences you can have as an adult. You'll be delighted again and again by the novel plots, the quaint coincidences and sometimes even the surprising insights about life that children will reveal in their make-believe play. You don't have to be a parent, either, to appreciate the benefits of collaborating on storytelling or pretend games with children. Whether you're a baby-sitter, a visiting uncle or aunt, a teacher, or a camp counselor, you'll be able to experience the thrill and warmth that come from children who are enjoying the development of their imaginative powers.

Life Enrichment
through Imagination

We all confront a stark tragic reality—the limited span of our life on earth. Clichés like "You only pass through here once" or "You only have one life to live" cannot conceal the inevitable frustration of our recognition that we must die. Devout Christians or Moslems may occasionally console themselves with the belief in an afterlife, although fewer people nowadays are likely to envision the Medieval Heaven of angelic choirs and piping cherubim. The yearning to surmount death is evident not only in the concepts of many world religions but also in the more recent scientific interests in flying saucers, UFO's and interstellar travel. Even the recent research on the psychology of dying—studies of persons on the threshold of death or of individuals who for a few seconds or minutes seemed clinically dead—have led investigators like Elisabeth Kübler-Ross to attempt to determine what's "beyond there."

Panoramic fantasies of Heaven or Hell expressed in the great poetry of a Dante or a Milton or in the paintings of a Michelangelo or El Greco have undoubtedly enriched the imagery of millions of people exposed to such art. The comic vision of Mark Twain led him to create "Captain Stormfield's Visit to Heaven," in which the deceased steamboat pilot finds that wings and harps are readily provided to all newcomers so as not to disappoint them but that they are soon discarded as unnecessary. Indeed, people in Twain's Heaven behave much as they do on earth (but without the responsibilities) and engage in a good deal of celebrity-chasing, turning out in large numbers for a chance to see a minor saint or an Old Testament patriarch.

A recent exemplification of the afterlife or beyond-life fantasy is presented in the movie, *Close Encounters of the Third Kind*. There, visitors from outer space are represented much like heavenly messengers, and the hero, arms outspread in crucifix-fashion, led by little children in an echo of the biblical phrase, goes aboard the mammoth spacecraft toward a mysterious alternative existence, which he hopes will be different from his current suburban lifestyle.

Whether or not you believe in the soul, transmigration, a resurrection, or other tenets, of organized religions, we believe that you can multiply the richness and value of your present life through the power of your imagination. The speed of thought and the privacy and flexibility of your imagery can permit you to live several lives at once, to travel through inner space and time, to associate with the great figures of history or fiction while you go about your daily business as shipping clerk, housewife, salesperson, college professor, or social worker. Actions and speech are very different from fantasies. If you do something directly, it has inevitable consequences; an insult to your spouse or the boss, a punch in the nose to a stranger who elbows past you on a ticket line cannot be "taken back." But you can engage in thousands of fantasies and even "get away with murder" if you rely on the privacy of imagery. We are suggesting, then, in the words of the chewing gum commercial, that you can "double your pleasure, double your fun"   **203** as you run your life course by allowing yourself to try out a variety of trips and lifestyles through your imaginative resources.

IMAGINATION, REMINISCENCE, AND OLD AGE

An elderly woman wrote a touching and sensitive letter to us after reading about some of the research on daydreaming. She lived in a small town in upstate New York and for some years had been confined to the immediate neighborhood of their small cottage because she was caring for an even older, bedridden woman.

"I think I would be utterly miserable with the monotony and loneliness of my daily routine," she wrote, "except for the daily trips I take in my imagination. Every afternoon I allow myself one hour or so during which I sit in an armchair and picture myself living in a villa in Florence, Italy. I see the pink-roofed house, the geraniums in the window boxes and in the clay pots along the path. I may work in the garden for a while amid the singing of the birds. Sometimes I walk down the hall to the street and cross the Arno River by the Ponte Vecchio and head up the hill to the Pitti Palace. I stroll through cool galleries looking at the paintings and at the lovely views of the city one sees from the palace windows. Then I meander slowly up through the Boboli Gardens to the Porcelain Museum and the panoramic view of the whole city and the Tuscan hills one gets there."

Mind trips of this kind can indeed be remarkably refreshing for many older people who can no longer get around so easily or who lack the resources for traveling. Retired persons, elderly widows or widowers often find they are slipping more and more into a kind of depressed apathy and bitter feeling of isolation. Older people in our society no longer have as many of the continuing responsibilities or leadership roles one found in the patriarchs or matriarchs of large extended families who lived together in the same rural farmhouse or ran the family shop that was so typical fifty years

204

ago or more. Important research by Professors Judith Rodin and Ellen Langer (of Yale and Harvard, respectively) has shown that very aged or enfeebled individuals in nursing homes can actually live longer if they are just given responsibility for caring for some plants. In some ways death comes not just when our body functions fail but is more likely when we lose interest in life. And travel, whether in reality or in fantasy, has an amazing restorative power because it provides us with novel sights, sounds, and social interchanges, a contact with history and art or adventure that can be quite exciting.

For the person who cannot undertake an actual trip, imagined ones can be worthwhile. Of course it's harder to carry out a visit to a place you've never seen. The way to develop such a trip is to begin by choosing a part of the world that especially intrigues you. Take a look at a map of the world and choose an area you'd like especially to explore. Then go to the library if possible or get someone else to help you locate some travel books about the area. Travel books usually include descriptions of a country, its history, its geography, the products its people grow or produce, what the architecture looks like. Any travel agent can supply you with brochures and pictures.

After you've seen some pictures of the setting and read about it, you might plan a very specific travel route. If you can locate or buy a very detailed travel itinerary book like the Michelin Guide for that area, it can help you pick out specific sights or works of art you might want to imagine. Then use your imagery to walk slowly through each of the locations, picturing scenes or people, thinking up conversations, little adventures like running into a little boy who talks English and whom you can ask about his family or his daily life.

Of course the mind trip isn't limited to old people by any means. It's a good way to broaden your horizons at any age. If you're young enough to be easily mobile, such explorations will whet

205

your appetite for actual travel and you might actually begin planning how to save your money and set up an actual trip. Realistically, however, most people will never get the money or time for trips to Tibet, New Guinea, or Tahiti so the mind trip can still be a delightful way of extending yourself.

Many older people also enjoy reminiscing about the past. This can be a very worthwhile form of daydreaming if it's done in an organized way. As a matter of fact, some research has suggested that giving senior citizens a chance to tell their life histories or to give detailed accounts of some of their experiences has an extremely valuable psychological effect. The success of television presentations like *Roots* and *Holocaust* has prompted younger family members from many cultural backgrounds to ask grandparents, parents, uncles, and aunts to tell more about family history. The wonderful *Foxfire* series of books in which high school students in Appalachia ask old people to describe the ways houses were built or hides tanned or to talk about old customs and rituals in detail has enriched our understanding of the past and has given older folks a greater sense of continued usefulness and responsibility. Couldn't we do more in every family or community by asking our senior citizens to think back more carefully about specific episodes in history in which they participated, places they saw, the kinds of work they did? As they do so, they will experience some sense of excitement in reliving experiences in imagination and also will gain an important, genuine sense of contributing to the continuity of society.

LIVING MULTIPLE
LIVES One way of enriching your life is to create some imaginary personalities or existences in other times or places. We've talked of children's imaginary playmates and how useful they can be in the growing-up process. But can't we all, *in fantasy,* allow ourselves some alternative lives or adven-

tures? It's true that there are a very small number of people, so-called "multiple personalities," who get into difficulties because they literally act out their fantasies of being someone else. The most famous cases are those of "The Three Faces of Eve" and "Sybil"; these women, who were rather over-controlled or inhibited but who had vivid imaginations of alternative ways of behaving, literally changed their personalities, forgetting who they were and behaving as if they were different people. But most of us need have no fears of such an occurrence if we approach a situation *playfully,* recognizing clearly that these are fantasies we can turn on or off as the outside world demands. Who hasn't, after all, daydreamed or wished that he or she might have a chance to experience some of the adventures or presumed glamour of a famous character in literature, history, or the movies? One of the co-authors, as a boy, developed extensive daydreams of being a baseball or football star. Such fantasies continue to be a source of enjoyment long after the "playing days" are past. You can replay old fantasies of winning games or think up new adventures for your heroes.

Think over your childhood or adolescence. Were there characters you admired from books, from sports, or from history? Perhaps you admired a famous violinist, jazz musician, or pop singer. Can you imagine yourself in his or her place, picture yourself singing or playing, traveling around the country, experiencing some sexual conquests or adulation from admirers? It's useful sometimes to allow yourself to develop a kind of alter ego, another personality you enjoy pretending to be. You can work up a series of adventures for this person and play them out in idle moments during long bus rides or waits in the optometrist's office.

Of course our society has for hundreds of years provided social outlets for persons to play out fantasies of another personality. Secret societies like the Masons or more public groups like the Elks, Moose, or Foresters gave farmers and craftsmen **207** opportunities to play at being important, different people with titles of nobility or magic. More recently, new kinds of groups have developed to help people elaborate private fantasies in a socially acceptable setting.

A surprising number of adults throughout America have become enchanted with reliving the Medieval or Renaissance past of Europe. Many assume roles of knights, noble ladies, scholars, or alchemists. Groups like the Society for Creative Anachronism meet regularly for medieval banquets with old dancing to ancient instruments, announcements in Latin, and much toasting with drinks like mead. A visit to a day-long assembly of one of those groups is like suddenly emerging from a time machine into the fourteenth century; there are round tents with pennants, knights in chain mail battling with short swords and maces (actually harmless rubber or plastic), large pigs roasting over burning coals, ladies with high-pointed hats cheering the jousters on, soothsayers and tumblers mixing in the crowd. Each of these participants has assumed a pretended identity not only for the actual meetings but also in his or her correspondence with others or in notes and articles they sent in to club newsletters. These people come from a wide variety of occupational and educational backgrounds and economic levels. They share with each other the opportunity to enjoy a separate life in a different century even as they go about their daily work as engineers, businessmen, teachers, or craftsmen.

Sometimes these alternative fantasies can be worked out around rather formal games. A history professor in New York leads a group of young adults who are replaying the Napoleonic era in Europe. Each becomes a character of the period, Marshal Blücher, the Duke of Wellington, General Murat, General Bernadotte, with the professor, naturally, playing Napoleon. They reenact battles with toy soldiers on a large board, planning elaborate tactics, discussing strategy, striving for historical accuracy and ingenuity in making their moves. Here, at least, one can say, "I'm Napoleon Bonaparte" without being hauled off to a mental hospital.

HEIGHTENING YOUR APPRECIATION OF LITERATURE AND ART

Not everyone can easily generate and sustain elaborate fantasies of adventure and social experiences. After all, we admire and reward that small number of gifted artists who can create in novels or short stories or in the other art forms fascinating characters, incidents, settings that transport us temporarily to another world. You can greatly increase your capacity to appreciate literature and art if you make a more active use of your imagery capacity. Too often people when reading hurry along at a rapid pace, grasping general plot and not allowing themselves the time to generate full images of the incidents or characters depicted. Even the most vivid and effective writer needs your help: careful reading and then filling out the words with your own private imagery. By reading a passage in a book and stopping to elaborate in your mind's eye the incidents presented, or by listening more carefully to the *sound* of the words and to the voices of the characters, you can be much more fully transported into the author's world.

A recent fine novel, *The World According to Garp* by John Irving, demonstrates this possibility. If you read the book carefully, allowing the characters to grow on you, vividly imagining Garp and his mother, his wife, the odd but lovable transsexual football hero, or other notable characters, you can be subtly led by the author into a remarkable emotional experience. The novel's climax comes when Garp, returning from an errand with his two sons in the car, cuts the car engine and coasts rapidly down his driveway, unaware that another car containing his wife and her lover in a compromising sexual situation is parked there. The chapter ends abruptly, leaving the reader wondering what happened. In the next chapter time has passed and

209

we are gradually filled in on the consequences of the crash, some horrible but also almost painfully funny. If we have allowed ourselves to be really caught up in the characters, we begin to be aware as the pages go by that something is missing. Details pile on details yet there is a nagging sense of puzzlement—why isn't Garp's younger son mentioned? We go back and reread the earlier pages; perhaps we missed something. Only after we have repeatedly experienced this tension—this silence—does the author reveal that after the accident, as Garp and his wife recovered their senses and became aware of the various gruesome details, they too experienced this strange silence and absence. Of course, it eventually becomes clear that the boy had been killed. By delaying his account of this event, John Irving has reproduced in the experience of the involved reader that same frightening, mysterious silence that finally alerted the Garps to the death of the child. It is a tour de force of literary skill but one we can appreciate most if we have truly been savoring in imagery the characters and incidents, living vicariously in the author's created world.

When we say that art enhances nature, we are in effect saying that opening ourselves to a fine painting or novel, replaying the imagery evoked at different times, can add a dimension of further richness to daily life or to new experiences. Hearing a nightingale singing in the darkness for the first time is a beautiful experience but it becomes even more haunting if we also are reminded of snatches of the poetry of Keats or Eliot.

What we are suggesting, then, is that using your imagery to the fullest when reading or watching a play or movie or television program can make a difference in your sense of daily wonder and excitement about life. You become the characters, if only briefly, but in a way you are having the best of many worlds. Of course, taking the time to allow your imagery to evolve and develop as you read may slow you down a bit. Recently Dr. Rollo

May (*Creative Living,* Winter 1979) has written about the importance of the *pause* in our lives. We need to *take time,* to step back, to savor experience or even, as in some forms of meditation, to briefly go beyond experience to a sense of oneness with our surroundings and our bodies. Daydreaming as you read gives you that kind of momentary sense of freedom from time and you can then move on in your reading having made the writer's world more fully a part of yourself.

Woody Allen, with his fine sense of taking some of our fantasies to their absurd extremities, has written a story about a man who so immerses himself in the novels he reads that he actually enters that world. In this case he finds himself so caught up in Flaubert's *Madame Bovary* that he can't find his way back from nineteenth-century provincial France. We have little to fear of such occurrences because our external world is very demanding indeed and we can return to it refreshed and excited after a good reading session.

In the ultimate sense, your powers of imagination bring out the most creative side of your personality. Creativity, after all, can be expressed not only in the production of a formal work of art, a symphony, a poem, a scientific invention. The free play of your memories, mingling together almost randomly as they do when you dream at night or allow your daydreams to drift along, provides all kinds of novel connections, some of which can be deeply meaningful, others just outrageously funny. Sometimes these are worth sharing with others as a starter for light conversations as well as for more serious probing.

One of the co-authors had a dream that went as follows:

"I meet a woman I haven't seen in a few years. Her name is Elsie Vanneman. Since we haven't been in touch, I hesitantly ask her about her husband. She says they're divorced and she is now married to a man named Horace Nyswanger. I ask her what name she plans to use since there are new

fashions today: will she keep her old name, actually her former husband's surname, or call herself
Mrs. Nyswanger, or go back to her maiden name,
or, as many people are doing now, hyphenate the
names and call herself Elsie Vanneman-Nyswanger
(which would be rather cumbersome). She replies
that she and Horace have decided that they should
start their marriage on a new basis, unencumbered
by names they had been given by others. They had
chosen a new name to symbolize the quality of
their marriage and their mutual ideals about life.
Henceforth they would be called Elsie and Horace
Whole-Wheat!"

Sharing this dream with others not only gets a
laugh but often does provoke an interesting discus-
sion about new trends not only in names but in
patterns of intimate relationships and family lifestyles. And who knows, maybe it's not a bad idea
after all for people's names to reflect their own
wishes and aspirations.

If you open yourself to the chance to live
more fully through your imagination, even if much
of your inner experience is not shared, you can
indeed extend the pleasure of life and, in a sense,
experience more each day. This openness to the
novelty and many-sidedness of yourself can also
be expressed in simple, practical ways, often without real planning. A woman we know was disturbed because small neighborhood children were
frequently throwing pebbles at her door or tramp-
ling her bushes. She called them together and gave
them an idea for playing an elaborate make-believe
game about knights and quests for dragons. Thus
she coped effectively with a minor daily life problem and also offered something constructive for
these children, who could then delight in the game
and teach it to others. Later on this woman, wondering why she'd suggested this particular game,
remembered that she had recently been reading
Barbara Tuchman's historic reconstruction of the
fourteenth century, *The Proud Tower*, and had
been vividly picturing some of the scenes of medieval tournaments.

Daydreaming is not likely to change your life in drastic ways. It is not a panacea for physical ills, racial or social oppression, nor will it resolve serious personal difficulties. It cannot provide an escape from the genuinely tragic realities of daily existence: the energy crisis, the suffering of the poor or isolated, the inevitability of death. Yet the acceptance, control over, and active use of your imagination can make it possible for you to explore potentials of your mind and body that can enrich your life in many ways. Even though we may rarely "act" on them, the fantasies and images we produce are very much a part of the reality of the human condition.

Bibliography

Wherever possible we have tried to base our proposals in this volume upon available research studies or clinical reports in the scientific literature. To avoid slowing the reader, we have omitted footnotes or citations of journal articles or books. The following is a brief annotated list of books which can provide detailed accounts of many of the experimental studies, research surveys, and clinical reports on which we have relied. Additional technical studies of effective uses of imagery are to be found in professional journals such as the *Journal of Mental Imagery, Cognitive Behavior-Modification, Journal of Consulting and Clinical Psychology,* and *Behavior Therapy.*

Barber, T. X. *LSD, Marijuana, Yoga and Hypnosis.* Chicago: Aldine, 1970.

An excellent review of scientific studies pointing up the interrelations between drug reactions, meditative and hypnotic states, and their common tie to suggestion and imagery. Includes a good review of the relationship of hypnosis to pain.

Klinger, E. *Structure and Functions of Fantasy.*
New York: Wiley, 1971.
A very technical, theoretical analysis of the scientific literature on the fantasy process.

Lazarus, A. (ed.). *Multimodal Behavior Therapy.*
New York: Springer, 1976.
A good, practical, clinically oriented presentation of a variety of behavior therapies, many of which depend a great deal upon imagery and fantasy.

Meichenbaum, D. *Cognitive-Behavior Modification: An Integrative Approach.* New York: Plenum, 1977.
A technical presentation of many methods for effective coping with daily stress and pain. Emphasis is upon techniques of "self-talking" and imagery.

Pope, K. S. and J. L. Singer (eds.). *The Stream of Consciousness: Scientific Investigations into the Flow of Human Experience.* New York: Plenum, 1978.

Singer, J. L., and K. S. Pope (eds.). *The Power of Human Imagination: New Methods in Psychotherapy.* New York: Plenum, 1978.
The above two volumes bring together highly technical theoretical and experimental research materials with very extensive bibliographies contributed by leading investigators of cognition, thought, and the clinical applications of imagery. Extensive reviews of the research bases for many of the concepts presented in the present book are available here.

Singer, J. L. *Imagery and Daydream Methods in Psychotherapy and Behavior Modification.* New York: Academic Press, 1974.
This book explores the historical and theoretical bases for application of imagery methods to clinical problems. It includes an examination of European Mental Imagery Methods as

BIBLIOGRAPHY

well as psychoanalytic and behavior modification approaches using imagery and fantasy.

———. *The Inner World of Daydreaming.* New York: Harper & Row, Colophon paperback series, 1975.

This book, written less technically, reviews research of the author and others on daydreaming and deals with issues, from investigations with adults and children, that underlie many of the assertions in the present volume.

Index

221

222

223